"*Becoming Gaia* is a path-b
er a wide range of creative
engaging vision of an integ
are few books as comprehe
insight. I trust it will inspir
for our urgent task—becoming part of the living Earth
community."

MARY EVELYN TUCKER, YALE UNIVERSITY, CO-AUTHOR,
Journey of the Universe

• •

"As we convulse our way into irreversible anthropocenic
harm, *Becoming Gaia* doesn't let us give up and give in.
Even mass extinctions and the possibility of our own do
not add up to The End. We are called to face, indeed to
embrace, the process as a collective death experience. Like
ancient rituals of initiation, of rebirth through fire and water, the dying can—may not but *can*—lead to a new birth:
a new Age of Enlivenment. Uninhibited by the limiting
dogmas of some environmentalism, Sean Kelly invites fellow humans beyond optimism and pessimism, to become
what we already are: living members of a vibrant Earth.
Always both practical and profound, this book pulses and
flows with the life of the planet."

CATHERINE KELLER, GEORGE T. COBB PROFESSOR OF
CONSTRUCTIVE THEOLOGY, DREW UNIVERSITY. AUTHOR
OF *Facing Apocalypse: Climate, Democracy and Other
Last Chances* and *Theology of the Earth: Our Planetary
Emergency and the Struggle for a New Public.*

"This book is an act of love. A reverence for reality underpins the integration of insight from diverse schools of thought. Whether ancient wisdom traditions or the latest science, Sean Kelly weaves together what is salient for our sense-making in times of great anxiety and disruption. In service of our own reconciliation with the predicament we are in, Sean shares the results of that sense-making. Whether you fully agree, or are inspired to find your own philosophical grounding, this book may nourish your journey as an expression of one consciousness, within Gaia, our planetary home."

JEM BENDELL, FOUNDER OF THE DEEP ADAPTATION MOVEMENT AND CO-AUTHOR OF *Deep Adaptation: Navigating the Realities of Climate Chaos.*

• •

"In *Becoming Gaia*, Sean Kelly has looked long and hard into the apocalyptic crisis of our time. He has brought all his courage, his rigorous intellect, and his compassionate care to the great task of forging a way to engage that crisis and to live into whatever future will now unfold. One might say that Kelly has taken the great bull of our age by the horns; but instead of doing so with the machismo of the bullfighter, he has looked deeply into its eyes, come into relationship with it, revealed its interior soul. With the aid of his major mentors and a pantheon of personal influences whom he lovingly invokes, he ends the book on an almost ecstatic note, setting forth the high spiritual vision that inspires him through the present darkness. Kelly has written a new *De Consolatione Philosophiae* for our time, a work both deeply learnéd and deeply confessional."

RICHARD TARNAS, AUTHOR OF *The Passion of the Western Mind* and *Cosmos and Psyche*

Becoming Gaia

On the Threshold of Planetary Initiation

Becoming Gaia

On the Threshold of Planetary Initiation

Sean Kelly

Integral Imprint
Olympia, WA
MMXXI

Becoming Gaia
On the Threshold of
Planetary Initiation

© 2021 Sean Kelly

Book and cover design by Jenn Zahrt.
Cover images by NASA/Goddard/Arizona State University

ISBN 978-1-947544-28-4
Printed globally on demand through IngramSpark

First printed in 2021 by INTEGRAL IMPRINT,
a REVELORE® imprint.

Integral Imprint/
Revelore Press
620 73rd Ave NE
Olympia, WA 98506

www.integralimprint.com
www.revelore.press

Contents

Acknowledgments

I am grateful to my editor, Jeremy Johnson, for his early and steadfast faith in my project and to producer, Jenn Zahrt, for her fine eye and lovely design; to Yuka Saito, Robert McDermott, Richard Tarnas, Brian Swimme, Jeremy Lent, Lisa Ferguson, and Linda Hess for their moral support and for helpful feedback on various portions of this text; to Jem Bendell for catalyzing my shift from incubation to writing; to my colleagues, Matthew Segall, Jacob Sherman, and Elizabeth Allison for their encouragement; and to Joanna Macy and Edgar Morin, both of whom have shown me what it looks like, even and especially in these end times, to love for the sake of life, and live for the sake of love.

Preface

I WRITE THESE LINES in the midst of the "Great Pause" occasioned by the global COVID-19 pandemic. An unprecedented hundreds of millions are sheltering-in-place as the captains of industry seek to return the global economy to the illusion of what was already a precarious equilibrium. I say "illusion" because the signs of approaching collapse have been accumulating for some time. As I make explicit in the concluding chapter of this book, we are living in end times. Even if, against all odds, we should succeed in slowing, if not halting, the accelerating mass extinction of species, even if we should avoid triggering the phase-shift into "Hothouse Earth", we stand poised on the threshold of what amounts to a planetary initiation with its own collective near-death experience (NDE). We cannot know what lies on the other side of this threshold. Perhaps all we can say with confidence is that, as Joachim of Fiore wrote almost a millennium ago, "We shall not be what we have been, but we shall begin to be other."

There are, to be sure, many individuals and communities already living this "other", many of whom are resisting business as usual, guided by their commitment to what Joanna Macy and others call the Great Turning to a life-sustaining society. At the core of this commitment is a recognition of our integral interbeing with Gaia, my preferred name for planet Earth, conceived and experienced not only as system but as community and subject in her own right.[1] It is in light of this integral interbeing

1. I am aware of the resistance in some quarters to referring to Earth as Gaia (see footnote 1. in Chapter 2), let alone as "She". While I could attempt to justify myself with reference to the many names for "Mother Earth" throughout human cultural history, I choose to speak of Gaia as "She" for two distinct, though

that I propose the term *Gaianthropocene* as an alternative to the now widely used *Anthropocene* to describe the new geological age we have entered into.

Our initiation into this new age, even as it threatens collapse and extinction, offers the possibility at least for greater actualization of spiritual ultimates. To accomplish this, however, requires that we not shy away from reflecting on these ultimates, that we take a stand on what we hold to be most true and good. In my own reflections, I continue to be inspired by Hegel's assertion that "The truth is the whole." The whole, he tells us,

> is merely the essential nature reaching its completeness through the process of its own development. Of the Absolute it must be said that it is essentially a result, that only at the end is it what it is in very truth; and just in that consists its nature, which is to be actual, subject, or self-becoming, self-development.[2]

Even if one is not able to follow Hegel in speaking of the Absolute, it is a remarkable fact that our end times coincide with the emergence of a near consensus regarding what can be known about the origins, history, and probable destiny of the cosmos, including especially

---

mutually reinforcing, reasons. First, in contrast to the dominant view of the Earth system as a mere collection of objects (however complexly organized) my own reading of this system's autopoietic or self-organizing character demands that Gaia be granted the status of *subject*, and indeed a kind of *hyper*-subject (taking my cue here from Timothy Morton's understanding of climate as a "hyper*object*"[Morton, 2010]). Secondly, while such a hyper-subject might very well transcend any human notion of gender, I have found, in harmony with the human cultural consensus over many millennia, that the feminine personal pronoun best suits my own psychospiritual experience of Gaia. The ground and implications of this experience are explored in Chapter 6.

2. Hegel, *Preface and Introduction to the Phenomenology of Mind, Edited*, with an introduction, by Lawrence S. Stepelevch (Macmillan/Library of Liberal Arts, 1990), 77 (par. 22).

the evolution of Gaia, our planet home. Though more speculative (and contested), there is a similar consensus among those scholars who concern themselves with such matters regarding the evolution of human consciousness. The latter includes not only world history as normally conceived, but deeper and more integral accounts of human development. As with the history of the cosmos, the history or evolution of human consciousness is a time-developmental process, which is to say that it has definite stages, a deep narrative structure with beginning, middle, and for those open to such considerations, some kind of end. Unlike the hypothetical end of the physical cosmos, however (with the currently favored scenario of universal "Heat Death"), the end of the evolution of consciousness, I maintain, is no mere terminus, but something in the nature of a *telos* or goal.

I suggest in the following pages that this goal be understood in relation to the ideal of concrete universality, the basic understanding of which I adapt from Hegel, but which is informed as well by other non-dual, integral, and complex insights. In contrast to the more abstract universality typical of the various spiritual ultimates articulated during the first Axial Age (with their emphasis on transcendence and their mutually exclusive claims to absolute truth), the second Axial Age unfolding in these end times is grounded in Gaia as embodiment of the concrete universal. Each chapter of this book strives to reveal something of the nature of this concrete universal, and thereby contribute to a more conscious participation in the "self-becoming" and "self-development" of Gaia— She in and through whom we have our being.[3]

---

3. Just as St. Paul (as quoted in *Acts* 17:28) felt free to adopt the words of two earlier Greek poets, which referred originally to the god Zeus, to characterize his faith in the living Christ, I have chosen to adapt them to my own faith in Gaia. The original lines of the poet-seer Epimenides (ca. 7th-6th century BCE) read:

The first chapter, "Gaia and a Second Axial Age," sets the context for what follows by outlining how we can understand the initiatory threshold on which the Earth community stands poised as the culmination of a mutation of consciousness which began some 2,800 years ago with the onset of the first Axial age. Building on my earlier work on the triphasic deep structure governing the birth and transformation of the Planetary Era, the second Axial age unfolding in our times is seen as the third phase of a single, organic process for which I propose the term *Axial Aion*.⁴ This third phase coincides with the dawn of the Gaianthropocene.

Chapter 2, "The Ethical Imperative of Big History," takes up the claim made in the first chapter that the new field of Big History has a key role to play in the self-understanding of the Earth community as it crosses into what Big Historians refer to as "Threshold 9". In contrast to the dominant voices in this field, which are generally wedded to a naïve materialist and reductionistic worldview, I offer a series of propositions to encourage

"But you are not dead: you live and abide forever,/ For in you we live and move and have our being." The next line in *Acts* is: "As some of your own poets have said, 'We are his offspring'." Here St. Paul is quoting the poet Aratus (3rd. century *bce*), the opening lines of whose work, *The Phenomena*, read:

> Let us begin from Jove [the Latin Zeus]. Let every mortal raise
> His grateful voice to tune Jove's endless praise.
> Jove fills the heaven—the earth—the sea—the air:
> We feel his spirit moving here, and everywhere.
> *And we his offspring are.*

4. My use of the term "Aion" should not be confused with the geochronological term "Eon", which refers to periods in Earth history spanning half a billion years or more. I am adapting the term "Aion" from Jung's reference to the "Christian Aion" (see Jung, *Aion: Researches into the Phenomenology of the Self [CW 9.2]*. Princeton UP, 1979) which corresponds to the roughly 2000 period from the birth of Christ to the turn of the third millennium. Similarly, the "era" in "Planetary Era" is not the geochronological "Era" which spans hundreds of millions of years, but a much shorter historical period (in this case, beginning around 1500 CE). The same holds true for my use of "age" and "period."

researchers to heed the ethical imperative of our times and to aspire not merely to knowledge, but to a genuine Gaian wisdom.

In the next chapter (3), "Cosmological Wisdom and Planetary Madness," I offer guidance for how Big History might ground itself in such wisdom. I do so by reexamining Thomas Berry and Brian Swimme's *Universe Story*—a foundational text in the emerging field of integral ecologies—by highlighting the deep structure of the cosmogenetic principle that informs their evolutionary narrative. The ecozoic ethical imperative that inspires this narrative is engaged through a consideration of how the three moments of the cosmogenetic principle can assist in understanding three related manifestations of planetary madness afflicting the Earth community in the dawning Gaianthropocene: climate chaos, mass extinction, and planetary apartheid.

Chapter 4, "Sources of the Good," turns to two other major figures in the field of integral ecologies: integral theorist, Ken Wilber, and complexity theorist, Edgar Morin. I bring the work of these two figures into generative dialogue around a cognitive meta-perspective that could inform an ethic for this critical phase of the Planetary Era. The same triadic deep structure at work in the cosmogenetic principle is in evidence with three main phases of the evolution of consciousness. Following consideration of the second phase of differentiation, which throughout modernity has passed into a pathological dissociation, I examine the complex-integral character of three principal sites of ethical engagement, three sources of the good: the individual, society, and nature/Earth. This prepares the way for reflection on a range of ethical imperatives for the Gaianthropocene.

The final two chapters return to the theme of planetary initiation. Taking my lead from some prescient observations of Richard Tarnas suggesting that the modern psyche is engaged in a collective rite of passage, Chapter 5, "The Paradox of Planetary Initiation," draws from the insights of transpersonal psychology, starting from the early founders William James and C.G. Jung, then in a sustained way from the perinatal theory of Stanislav Grof. I explore ways to apply Grof's observations on the archetypal nature of the death/rebirth experience to the highly charged dynamics of contemporary collective consciousness, confronted as it is with the prospect of mass extinction and civilizational collapse. Raising to consciousness the paradoxical quality of the planetary initiation that the Earth community is undergoing, awakening to the new Gaianthropic identity in the making, can allow for greater mutual understanding between activist communities caught between despair and hope, between those who believe that civilizational collapse and ecological catastrophe are inevitable and those still committed to the possibility of transitioning to some form of ecological civilization.

Even as it opens and abides with the fact that we do indeed live in end times, the final chapter (6) offers a series of reflections on the possibility of a third way, beyond both hope and despair. It is the most personal of the chapters. I allow my own voice to speak and appeal not only to data, concepts, and reasoned argument, but to lived experience, my own as well as that of others. It is also the most explicitly spiritual or metaphysical of the chapters in the tradition of what can be described as integral panentheism.[5] Invoking the experience of what

5. Where pantheism simply equates the all ("pan") or the cosmos with the divine ("theism"), pan*en*theism includes the idea that everything or the all is *in* ("en") the divine, just as the divine is *in* everything. My use of the term "integral" is largely inspired by the "integral non-dualism" of the Hindu sage, Sri Aurobindo, as well by the Swiss-German philosopher Jean Gebser's understanding of the "integral structure" of consciousness already evident in his times and which in many ways corresponds to my understanding of the second Axial Age. For

I call integral time, I propose the cultivation of a third kind of faith, a faith neither in otherworldly salvation nor in the fantasy of endless progress, but as an affirmation of the intrinsic and (truly) infinite value of the good, the true, and the beautiful, regardless of future outcomes. Even as we walk through the fires of planetary initiation, nourished in the wise and compassionate embrace of "wide-bosomed Gaia," we can answer Edgar Morin's call "to love for the sake of life, and live for the sake of love."

Sean Kelly
Berkeley, CA
May 2020

Sri Aurobindo, see Robert McDermott's *The Essential Aurobindo: Writings of Sri Aurobindo* (Lindisfarne Books, 2001), ; for Gebser, see Jeremy Johnson's *Seeing Through the World: Jean Gebser and Integral Consciousness* (Revelore Press, 2019).

1
Gaia and a Second Axial Age

We live in that time when Earth itself begins its adventure of conscious self-awareness.
— Brian Swimme and
Mary Evelyn Tucker

F OR THE FIRST TIME in sixty-six million years, with the accelerating mass extinction, global climate chaos, and increasing signs of civilizational collapse, the Earth community is being drawn into a collective, planet-wide Near-Death-Experience (NDE).[1] While NDES are known to occur spontaneously, they (or their experiential or symbolic analogues) have also been intentionally cultivated in all traditional societies as an essential moment of rites of passage or initiation. In all such rites, the initiation and its confrontation with death are not random events, but intentional processes, guided or lured by a specific goal. They are, in technical terms, teleological in nature (from *telos*: purpose, goal). For individual initiations, the purpose or goal involves the emergence of a new identity (whether of shaman, healer, chief, priest, warrior), an identity molded to serve the interests of the wider community. Something similar is happening in our times with regard to the threshold on which the Earth community now finds itself poised. In this case, however, we are dealing with the emergence of a radically new kind of identity or subject on a planetary scale. I use the word *Gaian* here as it seems, more than any other I have encountered, to be

1. See footnote 1. of Chapter 6 for a sample of relevant documentation.

a kind of strange attractor for many of the more creative manifestations of the emerging planetary identity.

Though accelerating in our own times, the emergence of this new identity has in fact long been in the making. Over two centuries ago now, Hegel announced that "ours is a birth-time and a period of transition to a new era. Spirit has broken with the world it has hitherto inhabited and imagined, and is of a mind to submerge it in the past, and in the labor of its own transformation...."[2] We are still in this period of transition, but the pace has quickened and the stakes are higher than Hegel could have imagined: not only the five-thousand year old fabric of civilization, but that of life itself on a planetary scale. With runaway climate change and the mass extinction of species well underway, we can legitimately say that we live in end times (*eschaton*). What kind of world awaits us on the other side of the eschaton depends upon how we navigate the next decade or so.

Hegel was not the first to announce the dawning of a new age. He stood quite consciously in a long line of prophet-seers, from his immediate Enlightenment predecessors (Kant, Condorcet), through the mystic Jacob Boehme and the pivotal figure of Joachim di Fiore, all the way to St. Paul and the "veil-lifting" (*apocalypsis*) claims of the New Testament.[3] I have argued elsewhere[4] that the birth and ongoing transformation of the modern period, or Planetary Era, is prefigured in certain central Biblical symbols which act, in Blake's expression, as the "Great Code" not only of art and literature, but of the deeper patterning of world history. Whether or not one agrees with my argument, one can perhaps grant the deep

---

2. G.W.F. Hegel, *The Phenomenology of Spirit* (Oxford UP, 1981), par. 12.

3. See Karl Löwith, *Meaning in History* (University of Chicago Press, 1949).

4. S. Kelly, *Coming Home: The Birth and Transformation of the Planetary Era* (Great Barrington: Lindisfarne Books, 2010).

resonance between our planetary moment and the New Testament's heightened sense of living in end times with a longing for a New Age.

The Christianity of the New Testament is a hybrid product of the earlier great transformation that Karl Jaspers termed the Axial Age. So much of what was to become the foundations of the world's great religions, major philosophies, and dominant worldviews were laid down from the 8th to the 3rd centuries BCE, the period Jaspers assigned to the Axial Age. With the near simultaneous emergence around the 6th century BCE of the first Greek philosophers (from Thales and Pythagoras to Plato), the Buddha, Mahavira, Confucius, and Lao Tzu, the great Jewish prophets (Second Isaiah, Ezekiel, Jeremiah), and possibly Zoroaster, this period "gave birth to everything which, since then, man has been able to be, the point most overwhelmingly fruitful in fashioning humanity." It is during this period "that we meet with the most deepcut dividing line in history. Man, as we know him today, came into being."[5] If Jaspers were alive today, he might see our own times as straddling "the most deepcut dividing line in history." He might as well have come to believe, as many do today, that we are witness to the dawning of a Second Axial Age.

Ewert Cousins was the first to present an extended treatment of the idea of a Second Axial Age.[6] He summarized his understanding as follows:

> Having developed self-reflective, analytic, critical consciousness in the First Axial Period, we must now, while retaining these values, reappropriate and integrate into

5. Karl Jaspers, *The Origin and Goal of History* (New Haven: Yale UP, 1968), 1.

6. According to Mary Evelyn Tucker (oral communication), the idea of a Second Axial Age was first proposed by Thomas Berry. Berry and Cousins were friends and colleagues at Fordham University.

that consciousness the collective and cosmic dimensions of the pre-Axial consciousness. We must recapture the unity of tribal consciousness by seeing humanity as a single tribe. And we must see this single tribe related organically to the total cosmos. This means that the consciousness of the twenty-first-century will be global from two perspectives: (1) from a horizontal perspective, cultures and religions are meeting each other on the surface of the globe, entering into creative encounters that will produce a complexified collective consciousness; (2) from a vertical perspective, they must plunge their roots deep into the earth in order to provide a stable and secure base for future development. This new global consciousness must be organically ecological, supported by structures that will ensure justice and peace. In the Second Axial Period this twofold global consciousness is not only a creative possibility to enhance the twenty-first century; it is an absolute necessity if we are to survive.[7]

The dominant strands of first Axial traditions tended to emphasize the transcendent pole in the vertical dimension (as we see in Platonic and the later Cartesian dualisms; Christian otherworldliness; Hindu and Buddhist views of the "wheel of life" as illusion or trap; in Chinese cosmology, the immovable Pole star as symbol of Heavenly power and virtue, or the Taoist immortals). In the extreme, according to Robert Bellah, these dominant strands involved "the religious rejection of the world characterized by an extremely negative evaluation of man and society and the exaltation of another realm of reality as alone true and infinitely valuable."[8] At the same time, while the first Axial Age involved a new consciousness

7. E. Cousins, *Christ of the 21st Century* (Rockport: Element Books, 1992), 10.
8. Quoted in J. Casanova, "Religion, the Axial Age, and Secular Modernity in Bellah's Theory of Religious Evolution," in *The Axial Age and its Consequences*, ed.

of the universal in its noetic, cosmic, and ethical dimensions, the several axial epiphanies of the universal remained rooted in the exclusive (ethno-linguistic) particularities of their respective culture spheres, and therefore in both of these senses the universal was abstract. "Great as the major figures of the axial age were," as Bellah would note in his last and greatest work,

> and universalistic as their ethics tended to be, we cannot forget that each of them considered his own teaching to be the only truth or the highest truth, even such a figure as the Buddha, who never denounced his rivals but only subtly satirized them. Plato, Confucius, Second Isaiah, all thought that it was they and they alone who had found the final truth. This we can understand as an inevitable feature of the world so long ago.[9]

A central task of the Second Axial Age, by contrast, involves the articulation of new forms of universality which could mediate between the particular culture spheres and help them confront their shared predicament: the threat of planet-wide ecological and civilizational collapse.

Despite the astounding synchronicity of the first Axial age, it was not global or planetary in extent, and its various representatives were largely unconscious of the parallel developments outside of their own culture spheres. At the same time, however—and as I have argued in detail in *Coming Home*—it was the destiny of one late hybrid shoot (Christianity) of this first axial mutation to become the symbolic catalyst or lure for the eventual emergence, some fifteen hundred years later,

R. Bellah and H. Joas (Cambridge, MA: Harvard UP, 2012), 194.

9. R. Bellah, *Religion in Human Evolution: From the Paleolithic to the Axial Age* (Cambridge, MA: Harvard UP, 2011), 602.

21

of the Planetary Era (more commonly designated as the modern period). It is with this specific genealogical line that we can discern an answer to the question of the relation between the two Axial Ages: The central symbols of Incarnation (of Spirit into matter, of the Logos into Cosmos, of the eternal into time) and of God as Trinity (the Absolute as internally differentiated) prefigure the deep structure of the movement from the first to the second Axial Age, with Modernity as the middle term between both Ages. The first Axial Age sets up the conditions of possibility for the eventual emergence of the second. These conditions include the reflexive and critical consciousness associated with "metacognition/theoretic culture" (Donald), the "disembedding" (Taylor) of culture from the cosmos and of the individual from the collective, and the lure of the universal (Voegelin, Assmann). At a deeper level, both ages can and should be seen as the two poles of a single process, or rotating axis, moving from the abstract to the concrete in three broad phases: 1. an initial identity (in this case, structured around the central myth/symbol of Incarnation wedded to the Greek intuition of the universal as logos/cosmos); 2. a movement of differentiation—and later, dissociation (leading to the birth of modern science, the modern disengaged subject, and the broader processes of secularization; all of which bring about the birth of the Planetary Era and the accelerating planetary crisis); 3. a new Gaian, or *Gaianthropic* identity in the making. The cultivation of this new identity is a central task of the Second Axial Age, which itself can be seen as the "opportune moment" (*kairos*) for the actualization of the deeper telos of what we can now discern as the 2,500-year Axial Aion. My proposal for the periodization of the larger arc that encompasses the two Axial Ages is as follows:

Axial Aion (c. 800 BCE to present):
First Axial Age (ca. 800–200 BCE)
Planetary Era (ca. 1500 CE to present)
Second Axial Age (Gaian epoch or **Gaianthropocene**)
(ca. 1945?-) [10]

My understanding of the Second Axial Age as coinciding with the Gaianthropocene and as the third phase of the (to date) 2,500 year Axial Aion is clearly speculative in nature. While all narrative accounts (and even mere chronologies) of our collective history involve some degree of framing, selection, and interpretation, mine is explicitly teleological in the tradition of such figures as Hegel, Jung, Teilhard, and Gebser. The distinctiveness of my account can be highlighted by considering two recent works, the short but instructive book, *The Axial Ages of World History*, by Baskin and Bondarenko,[11] and Bruno Latour's more substantial *Facing Gaia: Eight Lectures on the New Climate Regime.*[12]

While Baskin and Bondarenko do not say so explicitly, the authors suggest that the 21st Century marks the beginning of a *third* Axial Age. *Their* second Axial Age coincides with Modernity. All three Ages are seen as "thoroughgoing, transformational periods of crisis in world history" and share fundamental features and a common developmental pattern. Commenting on the first and second Axial Ages, for instance, the authors note:

> just as advancing literacy transformed the axial world, the printing press transformed the modern world; as

10. See Chapters 3 and 4 below for my proposal of the term *Gaianthropocene* as an alternative to *Anthropocene.*

11. K. Baskin and D.M. Bondarenko, *The Axial Ages of World History: Lessons for the 21st Century* (Litchfield Park: Emergent Publications, 2014).

12. B. Latour, *Facing Gaia: Eight Lectures on the New Climate Regime* (Cambridge: Polity Press, 2017).

iron reinvented axial manufacture and warfare, the machine did the same for moderns; and the modern experiments in democracy and totalitarianism, capitalism and nationalism served the same purpose as the social experiments in democracy and advanced bureaucratic government, socio-economic systems and identity building of the [first] Axial Age societies. All those experiments would unfold in both periods, as people relearned how to govern themselves in an increasingly complex social world that demanded they develop a different set of rules.[13]

The fundamental features shared by all three periods include the following six-part sequence: 1. Political fragmentation; 2. Social experiments grounded in foundational stories—a vision of cultural success based on its society's old world story; 3. Intensification of warfare; 4. Appearance of a new world story; 5. Developing commentary of that story, so that the society can amend its approach to unexpected challenges, and; 6. Emergence of empire.[14] I must refer interested readers to the text for details concerning these shared six features. The common developmental pattern they discern is characterized in very general terms in the language of dynamical systems where the Axial Ages represent "phase transitions" which punctuate more stable states.[15] In my understanding, as we have seen, the fundamental pattern of process or development (identity, differentiation, new identity) is expressed through the single, organic evolution of the Axial Aion from the first Axial Age, through Modernity, to the second Axial Age. Though both patterns are formally triphasic, the one I appeal to is teleological as well

13. K. Baskin and D.M. Bondarenko, *The Axial Ages of World History*, 2-3.
14. Ibid., 15.
15. Ibid., 98, 104.

as formal. It is not merely a case of paradigm shifts or of one worldview or system following upon the collapse of the previous one. In retrospect, at least—in the mirror of speculative recollection—we can discern in Gaia, and in the advent of the Gaianthropocene, something of the telos of the entire Axial Aion. From this perspective, instead of being an Axial Age in its own right, Modernity coincides with the phase transition between the first and second Axial Ages. This phase transition, however, though involving a negation of many constitutive assumptions of the first Axial Age (otherworldly transcendence, institutional and text-based authority, for instance), nevertheless shares the same commitment to the ideal of (abstract) universality.

It is in this sense that I interpret Bruno Latour's refrain that "we have never been modern." The first Axial Age and Modernity both give birth to forms of "natural religion" with a transcendent dimension based on the idea of an "Ordering God," for the former, and on the "Laws of Nature," for the latter.[16] Latour also has his own version of a third period, dominated by the "new climate regime" and the rise of Gaia as the "Third Estate." Though he does not appeal to the idea of Axial Ages, there are deep resonances between his evocation of the *Earthbound*—his name for humans in the Anthropocene—and my reading of the new Gaian identity in-the-making. In contrast to the abstract universals that dominated the first Axial traditions along with their partial negation (secularization) in Modernity, the new Gaian identity exemplifies the real-ideal of concrete universality.[17] This is where I take issue with Latour, however. Though I applaud him for choosing Gaia as the main theme of his Gifford

---

16. Latour, *Facing Gaia*, 173.

17. I adopt, and adapt, the term "concrete universal" from Hegel. In contrast to traditional notions of God as ground of universality (truth, goodness), for instance, where God is represented as standing beyond or outside of the cosmos,

Lectures, and though I find much of what he has to say insightful and generative, Latour's position falls short of the concrete universality demanded if we are not only to face Gaia, but to behold the true lineaments of her own remarkable face. In keeping with the still dominant forms of deconstructive postmodernism, Latour's Gaia has "no frame, no goal, no direction," no "unity, no universality...."[18] Gaia is "only the name proposed for all the intermingled and unpredictable consequences of the agents, each of which is pursuing its own interest by manipulating its own environment."[19] In the end, the "result of such a distribution of final causes is not the emergence of a supreme Final Cause, but a fine *muddle*. This muddle is Gaia."[20] Earlier in the text, Latour proclaims that "Gaia, the outlaw, is the anti-system."[21] Under the otherwise commendable desire to avoid the pitfalls of a totalitarian holism—which he associates with the spheres and globes of modern empires—Latour dogmatically asserts that, when it comes to Gaia, there are "neither parts nor a whole,"[22] and God forbid that we should think of Gaia as having a soul![23]

here the universal, as the Absolute or Whole, is conceived as fully actual only as including within itself and as embodied in the realm of physical and historical processes. While Spinoza's pantheism would identify God or the Absolute with Nature or the cosmos in its entirety, on pragmatic and existential grounds I take Gaia (or in mainstream terms, the Earth system) as the proximate incarnation of the concrete universal. "Planetary thinking," writes Edgar Morin, "ceases opposing the universal and the concrete, the general and the singular: The universal has become singular—it is the cosmic universe—it is the terrestrial universe." E. Morin with B. Kerne, *Homeland Earth: A Manifesto for the New Millennium* (New York: Hampton Press, 1999), 131.

18. Ibid., 107.
19. Ibid., 142.
20. Ibid., 100.
21. Ibid., 87.
22. Ibid., 95.
23. Ibid., 86.

I do not mean to judge Latour on the basis of his rhetorical flourishes (many of them quite brilliant). Given his considerable influence in contemporary environmental philosophy and in those circles engaged in serious and sustained reflection on Gaia, however, I feel obliged to offer a few more reflections, some appreciative and others more critical. To begin with, I take Latour at his word when he addresses the reader thus: "I beg you not to conclude that I am disdaining the ideal of universality: I recognize, share, I cherish this ideal. But I am seeking a *realistic* way to achieve it. And, to do so, we have to act as though we were certain that it has not *already* been realized."[24] I am in substantial agreement with Latour here. It is in this sense that I referred above to the "real-ideal" of concrete universality. It is a universal always in-the-making. It must, in Latour's terms, be *composed*. Responding to the facile epistemological critiques of climate sceptics, Latour notes that it is precisely because of the painstaking manner in which the findings of climate science are composed that they are compelling. "Instead of alternating abruptly between an impossible [abstract] universality and the narrow limits of their own point of view," he writes,

> it is because they extend their set of data from instrument to instrument, from pixel to pixel, from reference point to reference point, that they may have a chance to *compose* universality—and to pay the full price for this extension. The geologists, geochemists, and other geographers would be less schizophrenic if they agreed to call themselves Gaia-ologists, Gaia-chemists, and Gaia-graphers![25]

24. Ibid., 245.
25. Ibid., 215–16.

But if universality can be thus composed, why not also Earth or Gaia as system? If Latour reminds us that the objectivity of climate science consists in the fact that the communities of experts have "answered all the *objections* that could be raised against them,"[26] why reject the central organizing concept of system by means of which, along with the data, the objections have been answered? The consensus name for the multi- and inter-disciplines in question, after all, is Earth *system* science. The problem here, I think, is that Latour has allowed his laudable political resistance to all forms of domination to collapse the notion of the whole, of system, and totality into that of an a priori and totalitarian closure. Latour could, however, make a more consistent use of his suggestive notion of the world, and especially the world as Gaia, as a "metamorphic zone"—that is, a zone of "common exchange"[27]—where the bifurcation between Nature and Culture, object and subject, non-human and human, can no longer be sustained.

A more fruitful approach than the false dichotomy between system and anti-system, one that overcomes the bifurcations that have plagued Modernity along with the first Axial traditions out of which Modernity was precipitated, is represented by the integral ecological paradigm of complexity proposed by Latour's compatriot, Edgar Morin. Morin's understanding of the principles of the dialogic, recursivity, and holography as key ingredients of complexity allow for a non-reductive grasp of the relations between individuals, societies, and nature.[28]

---

26. Ibid., 47.

27. Ibid., 69.

28. See the works of Morin listed in the References; see also S. Kelly, "Integral Ecology and Edgar Morin's Paradigm of Complexity," in *The Variety of Integral Ecologies: Nature, Culture, and Knowledge in the Planetary Era*, eds. Sam Mickey, Sean Kelly, and Adam Robbert (Albany: SUNY Press, 2017).

One can celebrate the messiness, the complexity, of the many feedback loops studied by Earth system science without having to jettison in toto the specificity of the agents involved, whether these loops be between physical elements within the Earth system (hydrosphere, atmosphere, cryosphere, pedosphere, etc.) or between the physiosphere (Nature) and the anthroposphere (Culture/Society) which together constitute the more complex Gaian, or Gaianthropic (meta-)system. In order better to see, as Latour puts it, how "Gaia is indeed a third party in all our conflicts,"[29] we need something like the meta-point of view proposed by Morin. This meta-point of view is not the view from nowhere, the dominating, homogenizing, and globalizing gaze of Empire. Rather, it is an expression of the emergent transdisciplinary gaze of Gaia herself, reflecting herself not only as she is composed, but as we are composed by her in return. After all, what the countless acts of human composition reveal is that we are, as Latour says, thoroughly *Earthbound*.

A proper grasp of the complex (dialogical, recursive, holographic)[30] character of the relation of *physis* to *anthropos* is central to understanding Gaia as concrete universal. More obvious and arguably more fundamental than its socially constructed or composed provenance, the universality of Gaia consists in the fact that it is in and through Her that we live and have our being. Gaia is the *ground* of what we all share in *common* (a ground, moreover, that includes the sheltering atmosphere, which acts as a kind of subtle planetary amniotic fluid in which we are all suspended). For the same reason, this universality is concrete, to begin with, in the sense that the physical systems studied by Earth system science constitute the

29. Latour, *Facing Gaia*, 238.
30. I consider these three terms in more detail Chapter 4.

shared, living *body* of the entire Earth community. It is also concrete, however, in the specifically Hegelian and Morinian sense that it, or She, is *auto*-poietic or *self*-organizing (the foundational insight of Lovelock and Margulis' Gaia Theory), which is to say that Gaia is a *Subject* (as well as a communion of subjects—or agents, in Latour's terms—and not a mere collection of objects).[31]

The actualization of concrete universality that I see as the guiding spirit of the Second Axial Age will depend upon the successful coordination of multiple initiatives, both theoretical and practical, across the full spectrum of human endeavor. Here I will focus on some key features of the theoretical. If the First Axial Age was associated with the emergence of theoretic culture, with its second-order thinking or metacognition (that is, a reflexive thinking about thinking) and radical mythospeculation,[32] the Second Axial Age is marked by what could be described as third-order (participatory and re-embedded) metacognition and a new (planetary) radical mythospeculation. Integrating the critical, reflexive virtues of first-Axial theoretic culture, the leading edge of theory in the Second Axial Age recognizes the destructive potential of the disembedded, disengaged subject[33] (which reduces the world to a mere collection of objects). It re-embeds the human subject into the living Earth and cosmos—or

---

31. See the section on nature/Earth in Chapter 4.

32. I take the term "radical mythospeculation" from Robert Bellah (himself drawing on Eric Voegelin's idea of "mythospeculation") especially as it has been amplified by Richard Tarnas in his lectures and discussions in the Philosophy, Cosmology, and Consciousness program at the California Institute of Integral Studies. The term refers to the kind of creative hybridization of mythic narrative (story, metaphor and analogy) with reflexive theory (logical argument) which flourished during the first Axial age. It is "radical" in two senses: it mediates access to the realm of the transcendent or universal; secondly, this very access allows for and legitimizes a critical stance toward mere belief or received opinion. See Bellah, *Religion in Human Evolution*.

33. On the notion of the disengaged subject, see Charles Taylor, *Sources of the*

rather renews consciousness of the fact, and mystery, of its ontological consubstantiality with Earth and cosmos—which are now seen, celebrated, and engaged with as a communion of subjects. More radically, we can say that the radiating center of the second Axial Age is constituted by an awareness in a growing network of individuals and communities that "We live in that time when Earth itself begins its adventure of conscious self-awareness."[34]

In the variety of Big History associated with David Christian, Earth or Gaian evolution is conceived as currently poised on "Threshold 9" (the previous eight thresholds are: 1. origin of universe; 2. formation of stars and galaxies; 3. formation of heavier chemical elements; 4. formation of Earth and the solar system; 5. emergence of life; 6. birth of *homo sapiens*; 7. agricultural revolution; 8. the modern revolution (or what I call the Planetary Era). Christian has little to say about the new evolutionary threshold (#9), other than underlining its radically uncertain character (which in any case attaches to the emergent properties associated with all new thresholds) and the possibility, at least, of somehow achieving a sustainable planetary civilization. Futurist and Big Historian Joseph Voros concludes soberly that the most likely path ahead involves "a slowly-unfolding collapse or 'descent' over a time-scale of decades-to-centuries towards a human society characterized by ever-declining access to sources of fossil fuel-based energy."[35] At the same time, however, drawing from fellow futurist James

Self: The Making of the Modern Identity (Cambridge, MA: Harvard UP, 1989/1996).

34. B. Swimme and M.E. Tucker, Journey of the Universe (New Haven: Yale UP, 2011), 109.

35. J. Voros, "Profiling 'Threshold 9': Using Big History as a Framework for Thinking about the Contours of the Coming Global Future," in *Evolution: Development within Big History, Evolutionary and World-system Paradigms*, eds. L.E. Grinin and A.V. Korotayev (Volgograd, Russia: Uchitel, 2013).

Dator's fourfold typology of alternative futures,[36] Voros leaves open the possibility of Threshold 9 involving an eventual transition to a planetary "transformational society," visions of which tend to emphasize either technological breakthroughs or the actualization of spiritual potentials (the other three possible futures are: continued growth, collapse, and "disciplined society"). In the latter case, "some new form or aspect of human consciousness emerges and redefines our value systems, such that we become focused on 'higher' goals than we currently pursue." It might be argued, he continues, "that Cosmic Evolution, Big History and other related conceptual frameworks may themselves provide a foundation for a new more integrated worldview, onto which an almost spiritual dimension could be read."[37] Clearly what I am proposing in terms of the emergence of a new Gaian or Gaianthropic identity qualifies as such a new, radical transformation of consciousness.

This transformation is informed and catalyzed by many distinct, if overlapping, disciplines, including Earth System science, Big History, the various strands of ecological science and environmental studies, the field of religion and ecology, and the emerging transdiscipline of integral ecology. For present purposes, I would single out the generative contributions of Thomas Berry, one of the founders of integral ecology and, along with Brian Swimme, Mary Evelyn Tucker, and others, bard or prophet of a more coherent and inspiring Big, or better, Deep History. "We need to think of the planet," Berry writes, "as a single, unique, articulated subject to be understood in a story both scientific and mythic [and, I would add, ethical and

---

36. See C. Bezold, "Jim Dator's Alternative Futures and the Path to IAF's Aspirational Futures," *Journal of Futures Studies* 14.2 (2009): 123–34.
37. Voros, "Profiling 'Threshold 9.'"

political]."[38] I will consider Berry and Swimme's version of deep history in greater detail in Chapter 3.

Returning to the theme of initiation with which I opened this chapter, we can note that an essential component during the liminal ("threshold") phase of many rites of initiation involves introducing the initiate to the sacred stories, myths, and symbols of the community into which they are being inducted. In contrast to the situation in both archaic or indigenous societies and in first Axial traditions, the stories and symbols required for this collective initiation into a new Gaian identity need to include a genuinely common narrative core, regardless of language and ethnicity. The only candidate in this case is the Universe story itself, the major lines, phases, and thresholds of which are, for the first time in the history of our species, well understood and universally acknowledged by the many scientific communities devoted to their study. This is not to say that there is no longer a place for the stories, myths, rituals, and doctrines of the world religions and of indigenous cultures. On the contrary, these should continue to provide inspiration for reflection on the mysteries of the cosmos, of human nature, and the question of spiritual ultimates, including indications of how we might best navigate the critical planetary threshold on which we are so precariously poised. It is precisely to this end that so much fine work is now being done in the field of religion and ecology.[39]

Of course, we cannot know, or at least we cannot expect to arrive at a general consensus as to whether or not one or the other of the world's religious traditions might actually have a direct line to the Universal (or Universals)

38. T. Berry, *The Sacred Universe: Earth, Spirituality, and Religion in the Twenty-First Century* (New York: Columbia UP, 2009), 112.

39. See J. Grim and M.E. Tucker, Ecology and Religion (Washington, DC: Island Press, 2014).

intuited during the first Axial Age. We can and must, however, acknowledge the sacred or enchanted character of Gaia as concrete universal. The story of Gaia is sacred because it tells of our common origin and will include our shared destiny. We can therefore envision the open spaces of this living Earth, in and through whom we literally have our being, as the Common Temple of the Second Axial Age, with the sacred places explored by the world's religious traditions as so many side temples with their own unique paths leading to the great Mystery.

It is possible that a new, third kind or species of religion might emerge from our gathering in the sacred precincts of this Common Temple. As Edgar Morin puts it, this would be religion "in the minimal sense"[40] of the term (suggested in one derivation of the word: from *re-ligare*: to join back together), at the heart of which would be the fact and ideal of planetary "re-liance" (which we can understand as the binding force behind Latour's notion of the "Earthbound"). While the first kind of religion arose out of the first Axial Age, and the second kind in the Modern period with its faith in this-worldly salvation (the myth of Reason, of progress and "development"), the new religion, by contrast,

> would not have promises but roots: roots in our cultures and civilizations, in planetary and human history; roots in life; roots in the stars that have forged the atoms of which we are made; roots in the cosmos where the particles were born and out of which our atoms were made.... Such a religion would involve belief, like all religions but, unlike other religions that repress doubt through excessive zeal, it would make room for doubt within itself. It would look out onto the abyss.[41]

40. Morin and Kerne, *Homeland Earth*, 141.
41. Ibid., 142.

The Earth community is being dragged to the edge of this abyss. Faced with the prospect of ever more probable civilizational collapse and an accelerating mass extinction, the human members of this community must learn to think, feel, and act out of their wider and deeper identity as Gaia. There is no guarantee that we will avert planetary catastrophe. There never has been such a guarantee. We might still, however, accomplish the task that has been the secret preoccupation of the 2,500-year Axial Aion, if not of the 4.6-billion-year journey of Earth's evolution.

2

The Ethical Imperative of Big History: Toward a Gaian Wisdom

Gaian science...can thus be distinguished from Earth System science by its striving to bring a sound science of the Earth together with ecological wisdom and action.
—S. Harding

W E SAW IN THE PREVIOUS CHAPTER that the new field of Big History, as one author has claimed, might provide "a foundation for a new more integrated worldview." The field of Big History traces its formal origins to the work of David Christian (2005), who coined the term. In fact, however, classics in the field include Swimme and Berry's *Universe Story* (1992, which I will turn to in the next chapter), Teilhard de Chardin's *Human Phenomenon* (1955/1999), Carl Sagan's *Cosmos* series (1980), Jacob Bronowski's *Ascent of Man* (1973), and much earlier works, including especially von Humboldt's *Cosmos* (1845), and the early 19th-century works of Lorenz Oken and Schelling, among others. I realize that the field of Big History is not monolithic, that there is no formal dogma and no official imprimatur, and that real efforts have been made to erect and maintain the movement's "big tent." At the same time, it is my impression that certain presuppositions remain dominant, if not always explicitly stated—namely, that Big History should abide by the modernist strict separation of facts from values; that accounts of the cosmos and of the human within the cosmos should be couched in purely objective terms; and that, in particular, the overarching narratives of Big History should eschew questions of meaning or purpose. The following reflections, by contrast, invite the reader (and more particularly, the partisans of Big History) to consider the possibility that our current planetary predicament demands that we challenge such presuppositions. With civilization and complex life itself in the balance, I suggest that Big History is charged with an ethical imperative explicitly to seek not only knowledge, but wisdom. What follows are a series of sometimes intentionally provocative propositions which together can be taken as a kind of manifesto for those Big Historians open to the ethical imperative of our planetary moment.

* * *

1. The time elapsed since the emergence of a planetary humanity, the most recent threshold crossed in our neighborhood of the evolving cosmos, is quantitatively insignificant relative to the cosmic time-scale, yet its qualitative significance, in both theoretical and practical terms, is paramount. Runaway climate change, loss of habitats, and the sixth mass extinction of species underway signal the potential unraveling of the fabric of life, and with it, the human organizational complexity that allowed for the rise of Big History in the first place. The shift in perspective from quantitative scales to the qualitative singularity, and criticality, of our moment invites us to engage in deep questioning about the goal of evolution, the nature of the good, and of our ultimate concern.

2. If humanity is to succeed in making the transition to the next threshold (Threshold 9, as many refer to it) of complexity toward a truly sustainable Earth community,

civilization will need to be regenerated along Gaian lines. Human social, economic, technological, and political activities must become synergistic with the principles of planetary ecology. Gaian or Earth System science[1] has

1. "And Gaia, what about Gaia?," asks professor emeritus of geophysiology, Peter Westbroek. "When you look through the literature you can hardly find a trace of it. Research on Gaia is OK, but do not mention that name if you want a job! Gaia is taboo. The scientific inquisition is watching you. With the primacy of physics evaporated and global biology on its way, what else is standing in the way of Gaia? The problem is epistemology." Quoted in B. Clarke, "Autopoiesis and the Planet," in *Impasses of the Post-Global: Theory in the Era of Climate Change*, vol. 2, ed. Henry Sussman (Ann Arbor: University of Michigan, 2012).

While the situation may be improving, I too have encountered considerable resistance among some big historians to the term Gaia because, as one anonymous reviewer of this text remarked, "of its association with teleology and purpose, which most scientists disavow. We use instead the term 'Earth systems,' which we strongly favor." While individuals are of course free to use whatever term they see fit, the question of teleology or purpose is a matter of legitimate debate. Here I would make the following two points: first, the term Gaia is by no means absent from the scientific literature, as one sees not only with Lovelock's foundational writings, but for instance with the authoritative collection of 53 articles edited by S. Schneider, et al., *Scientists Debate Gaia: The Next Century* (Cambridge: MIT Press, 2008) and the 19 articles edited by E. Crist and H.B. Rinker, *Gaia in Turmoil: Climate Change, Biodepletion, and Earth Ethics in an Age of Crisis* (Cambridge: MIT Press, 2010). My use of the term might be characterized in terms of what Stephan Harding calls "participatory holistic" science. Most research in Earth System Science, though also holistic, is "detached." "It is not too far-fetched," writes Harding, "to imagine that some Earth System scientists could see the Earth as a mechanism, albeit a hugely complex one, with instrumental value insofar as it provides 'ecosystem services' for sustaining human interests, and particularly continued economic growth." Gaian scientists, by contrast, "recognising that science cannot and should not be separated from moral, political and economic concerns, seek to deeply question and remould themselves and society based on their deep experiences of studying, living in and identifying with Gaia.... Gaian science...can thus be distinguished from Earth System science by its striving to bring a sound science of the Earth together with ecological wisdom and action." S. Harding, "Earth System Science and Gaian Science," *Earth System Science. Proceedings of the International School on Earth and Planetary Sciences* (Siena: University of Siena, 2001), 227–33. Schumacher College, https://www.schumachercollege.org.uk/learning-resources/earth-system-science-and-gaian-science.

An impressive articulation of a comprehensive model of Earth System science which makes room for teleology and purpose is represented by the work of leading climate scientist Hans Joachim Schellnhuber, founder and chairman

a leading role to play here in alerting us to key guiding principles, as do the related insights of Big History,
which provide the longer-term perspective. In both cases,

of the Potsdam Institute for Climate Impact Research and a leading European
climate scientist. What is striking in his model is the inclusion of factor "S" as
the "global subject," a "metaphysical dimension" explicitly concerned with the
pursuit and production of value and meaning:

> At the highest level of abstraction, the make-up of the Earth system E
> can be represented by the following "equation":
>
> $$E = (N, H) \quad (1)$$
>
> where $N = (a, b, c, ...)$; $H = (A, S)$. This formula expresses the
> elementary insight that the overall system contains two main components,
> namely the ecosphere N and the human factor H. N consists of an alphabet
> of intricately linked planetary sub-spheres a (atmosphere), b (biosphere),
> c (cryosphere; that is, all the frozen water of Earth), and so on. The human
> factor is even more subtle: H embraces the "physical" sub-component A
> ("anthroposphere" as the aggregate of all individual human lives, actions
> and products) and the "metaphysical" sub-component S reflecting the
> emergence of a "global subject.' This subject manifests itself, for instance, by
> adopting international protocols for climate protection. [...]
>
> Global environmental change is all around us now, and the material
> components of the Earth system, N and A, are behaving like a strongly
> coupled complex. [...]
>
> But H embraces a second sub-factor, S, which makes all the difference.
> This entity, introduced as the "global subject" above, represents the collec-
> tive action of humanity as a self-conscious control force that has conquered
> our planet. The global subject is real, although immaterial... [...]
>
> The Global Subject transcends the sum of the physical-individual
> desires and impulses of all elements of A as a result of a self-referential pro-
> cess. The collective target structure emerges through million-fold communi-
> cation, perception and evaluation of personal value-systems as a synergistic
> control quantity (for physical metaphors like mean-field theory see e.g.
> Negele, 1982 [164]; Haken, 1983 [96]; Baxter, 1990 [16]; Landau, 1996 [128]).
> One element of this target structure might, for instance, be the intention of
> limiting anthropogenic warming of the Earth's atmosphere to a maximum
> of 2°C—a project that would profoundly shatter and revise the respective
> manoeuvring spaces for individual action regarding energy consumption,
> mobility, etc. in every respect. This means, however, that in the Earth Sys-
> tem—besides N and A—yet another entity exists, which manifests itself in a
> "metaphysical dimension."

H.J. Schellnhuber, "Discourse: Earth System Analysis—The Scope of the Challenge," 23, http://edoc.gfz-potsdam.de/pik/get/1224/0/15809de6c77a70f38cb-
34da38db533f6/1224.pdf.

however, the urgency of our planetary moment demands that we grapple with ideas, and ideals, that transcend the traditional limits of science-based inquiry: these include Earth justice and Earth law (including the rights of nature and proper relations to the global commons), Gaian governance, and more broadly what might be recognized as Gaian wisdom.

3. A major goal of Big History is to provide a more comprehensive cosmological and evolutionary context for the human project. One initial effect of the vast time scales of this contextualization is the diminishment of the human to quantitative insignificance. Given what many consider to be a misguided and pernicious anthropocentrism, such a diminishment could be considered a virtue. At the same time, if there is any merit to the notion that Earth has entered a new geological epoch, such quantitative diminishment must be coupled with the recognition of a qualitative singularity. While all major evolutionary thresholds (Big Bang, ignition of stars, origin of life, collective learning, agriculture, the modern revolution) are in some sense singular, the current moment presents us with an unprecedented bifurcation point. The closest parallel is the Cretaceous-Paleogene mass extinction event of 66 million years ago. The mass extinction now underway (coupled with climate change and habitat loss), however, involves not only the unraveling of complex life on Earth—which of course is the most fundamental threat—but also the unraveling of subsequent thresholds of complexity, especially the core elements of the modern civilizational revolution, along with the conditions for terrestrially coordinated collective learning.

4. The qualitatively singular context of human existence, and therefore also of the project of Big History, is the current, accelerating planetary crisis. One direction leads

further into the planetary great unraveling. The other direction points to what Joanna Macy, David Korten, and others call the Great Turning toward a truly Gaian civilization. The word "Gaian" here suggests, following the lead of James Lovelock, a dynamically stable, self-regulating planetary system capable of sustaining maximally diversified complex life, including the human! "Civilization" indicates the desire to preserve not only the biological complexity of the human genome, but human cultural depth and diversity as well.

5. The emergence of a Gaian consciousness—including not only knowledge of Gaia's probable genesis and evolution, but also an understanding of the complex character of the later modern, or (as I prefer to call it) Planetary era and the integral role of the human in the history and fate of this era—represents the latest and most complex evolutionary threshold of which we have any evidence. It is also the first threshold to make explicit the cosmological truth that each evolutionary threshold, or the representative systems associated with those thresholds, include as they transcend the levels of organizational complexity attained by the previous systems. This truth is made theoretically explicit through Big History-type narratives, which typically include such insights as how living organization is metamorphosed stardust, or how human cells preserve evidence of symbiogenetic mergers of simpler organisms, or how modern humans preserve genetic markers from our common mother, "mitochondrial Eve." As noted above, however, this truth is also practically evident in the fact that human behavior is now the critical deciding factor in the question of whether or not the majority of our elder cousins (among the complex organisms, at least) on the tree of life will survive into the next century.

6. To be true to the qualitative context of our planetary moment, some big historians, at least, will need to concern themselves with some of the big questions previously reserved for philosophers and theologians. Along with the question of the origin and evolution of the cosmos, Earth, and the human, those of us with the privilege of being able to do so must also ask the question of "the good life," of how we ought to live, not only in general terms, but relative to the here and now of our planetary predicament.

7. Clearly, any adequate engagement with the big questions will need to draw not only from multiple disciplines, including the sciences (natural and social) and humanities as currently constituted, but also from more transgressive modes of inquiry that mix, cross, and even transcend the disciplines as normally conceived, such as mythically/imaginally inflected narratives and transdisciplinary (meta)points-of-view. While still devoted to truth, serious inquiry can no longer in good faith style itself as "disinterested". There is a residue of value (and of feeling, intuition, symbol) in the most stubborn of facts, and more than a residue in the most tested of theories. The more comprehensive, or "Big" the theory, the more we can expect this to be the case. While Big History is not, strictly speaking, a theory, it is a way of seeing or "viewing" (from the Greek, *theorein*) things, and not just some things, but everything! It is therefore the most egregious form of performative contradiction if, in attempting to think the Whole, one would persist in the modernist fantasy of a "pure," "disinterested," and "objective" account of the cosmos, uncontaminated by such things as meaning and value (not to mention metaphors, symbols, and even myths). Not only have philosophers of science (Whitehead, Kuhn, Holton, Feyerabend, among others) long recognized as much, but so too have the

most creative of the scientists themselves (Einstein, Bohr, Schroedinger, Pauli, Bohm, Prigogine, to name some of the most prominent).

8. What this means is that the knowledge pursued, produced, and promulgated by Big Historians should at some point be explicitly yoked to the ideal of wisdom, in both its theoretical and practical modalities. In neither case is there room for claims to absolute truth or certainty, though individuals are of course free to argue the coherence or adequacy of any account that claims, explicitly or not, to be not only in some sense true, but wise and good.

9. Bracketing the question of metaphysical absolutes, we might at least agree on the value of focusing our gaze on Gaia, our planet-home, as the concrete universal or proximate context of our cosmic and anthropological being, our origin and destiny. Honoring this context, the project of Big History would embrace the ethical imperative to resist the forces—social, economic, political, ideological, psychological, spiritual—contributing to the Great Unraveling and instead devote itself to the Great Turning towards a truly Gaian civilization. Along with this resistance, the ethical imperative of Big History, in service to the Great Turning, requires the cultivation of a Gaian wisdom. Again, while abjuring any claims to absolute truth or certainty, the broad outlines, at least, of such a wisdom can be proposed.[2]

10. Theoretically, such a wisdom would be grounded in a Gaia-centric evolutionary narrative of suitably trans-

2. I have made some preliminary suggestions to this effect in Kelly, *Coming Home*. See especially Chapter 12, "First Light: Toward a Planetary Wisdom Culture".

disciplinary depth and scope. Going further and deeper than mere inter- or multi-disciplinarity, the transdisciplinarity of Big History would seek to bring to conscious awareness the root metaphors and otherwise unconscious paradigmatic assumptions (such as mechanistic or reductive naturalism) that not only structure but often limit the creative (and moral) imagination. It would deepen its already acute attention to contexts (cosmic, social, cultural, planetary) in all of their complexity. It would relinquish, once and for all, the idea of a "view from nowhere," and therefore reintegrate the subject/observer in its consideration of all objects and matters of fact.[3] It is

3. An example of the kind of object/subject and fact/value dissociation that no longer serves can be found in the following statements of distinguished astrophysicist and Big Historian, Eric Chaisson:

> Why do so many big history advocates associate natural events with "purpose," "progress," "magic," and "meaning," all of which slippery words are anathema to most physicists who feel they do not aid objective understanding of our material universe?
>
> Will big history rise to the challenge of genuinely embracing modern science's central dogma, thereby accepting the need to test ideas while soundly rejecting those that go untested....
>
> If big historians are to base their awe-inspiring, interdisciplinary story on the empirical evidence of modern science, then they ought to accept some objective, quantitative reasoning without recourse to pseudo-scientific nonsense and without pandering to those clinging to antiquated subjectivity. (E. Chaisson, "Big History's Risk and Challenge," Expositions 8.1 [2014]: 85–95, https://www.cfa.harvard.edu/~ejchaisson/reprints/Expositions_BH.pdf.)

In this connection, Harvard Professor, David Armitage remarks that:

> Big history in all its guises has been inhospitable to the questions of meaning and intention so central to intellectual history. This is not simply for the banal reason that the big historians usually scrutinize such a superficial slice of recorded history at the end of their grand sweeps: the skin of paint on the top of the Eiffel Tower, in Mark Twain's marvellous metaphor. Nor is it just because human agency dwindles in significance in the face of cosmological or even archaeological time. It is due, for the moment at least, to the essential materialism of the two main strains of big history, what we might call the biologistic and the economistic tendencies.
>
> The biologistic tendency is neurophysiologically reductive: when

not a question here of falling into a purely constructivist hall of mirrors, but rather of cultivating a sustained re-flexivity in thinking, especially when striving to think the whole, whether this be the wider cosmos or the concrete universal of Gaia, our planet-home.

11. The reintegration of the subject is not only theo-retically but practically necessary for the cultivation of wisdom. Practical wisdom demands that science recover its con-science. To begin with, this will involve the recog-nition that, just as all facts are theory-laden, so theories (or accounts of what is the case, how it became such, or why it is such) and the choice or articulation of research problems are value-laden, which is to say that they have ethical consequences for humans and the world we inhabit. Being true to the facts is not a matter of mere re-porting, but of commitment to the matter at hand, which for all of us now is the planet in peril, with civilization and complex life itself in the balance.

12. Though Big History is not itself a science, if it is to be true to the facts and committed to the matter at hand, if it is to affirm the ideal and practice of science with a conscience, it will need to make room for and even encourage consideration of the teleological dimension—

all human actions, including thought and culture, can be explained by brain chemistry, reflections approximate to reflexes. In the economis-tic strain, intellect is assimilated to interests. Each age simply "gets the thought that it needs." For instance, whether it's Buddhism, Christianity or Islam in the Axial Age, it's all the same in the end: simply the product of the problem-solving capacity of some rather clever but needy chimps. In these regards, at least when it treats the questions of most concern to intellectual historians, deep history can appear to be somewhat shallow. (D. Armitage, "What's the Big Idea? Intellectual History and the Longue Durée," *History of European Ideas* 38.4 (2012): 493–507, http://dx.doi.org/10.1080/01916599.2012.714 635.)

that is, the dimension of value, meaning, purpose, and goals—as intrinsic to any sufficiently complex and truly transdisciplinary account of both cosmos and anthropos. In practical terms, such consideration would include, and be guided by, the commitment to a just and sustainable, if not flourishing, Earth community. Proponents of Big History, in other words, cannot in good conscience remain silent on matters of politics, economics, and social policy. The ethical imperative of Big History calls for its advocates to take a stand on all matters that touch upon the growing threat to the planet's biosphere.[4] The

4. "Within the scientific community," Schellnhuber said on the occasion of the publication of the Papal encyclical, *Laudato Si'*, "there is almost a code of honor that you will never transgress the red line between pure analysis and moral issues." "But we are now in a situation where we have to think about the consequences of our insight for society." J. Yardley and L. Goodstein, "Pope Francis, in Sweeping Encyclical, Calls for Swift Action on Climate Change," *New York Times*, June 18, 2015, https://www.nytimes.com/2015/06/19/world/europe/pope-francis-in-sweeping-encyclical-calls-for-swift-action-on-climate-change.html. Prominent glaciologist Dr. Jason Box has remarked that "most scientists must be burying overt recognition of the awful truths of climate change in a protective layer of denial (not the same kind of denial coming from conservatives, of course). I'm still amazed how few climatologists have taken an advocacy message to the streets, demonstrating for some policy action." J.H. Richardson, "When the End of Human Civilization Is Your Day Job," *Esquire*, July 20, 2018, https://www.esquire.com/news-politics/a36228/ballad-of-the-sad-climatologists-0815/.

Does my invocation of the ethical imperative of Big History mean, as I have been asked, that those who include Big History in public school curricula, for instance, should take "overt stands on specific political issues"? If the issues in question involve the imminent threat of biospheric collapse (through catastrophic runaway climate change and mass extinction), my answer would be, Yes! The consensus among relevant experts, for example, is that 90% of existing fossil fuel reserves must stay in the ground if we are to have a chance at limiting global warming to 2C above preindustrial levels. Along with the promotion of green energy initiatives, the case seems very strong that concerned citizens (including scientists, historians, academics and educators in general, and all those in positions of influence) should speak out in favor of the movement to divest from fossil fuels. Where there is less consensus or even active contention around specific policies or proposed actions (such as with GMOs or solar radiation management, for instance), such individuals ought, to my mind, make their views clear and invite debate with the goal of arriving at, if not consensus, at least greater collective understanding of the issues in question.

question here is one not only of survival, but of justice on a planetary scale. It is a question of Earth justice, which recognizes the intrinsic right—in the sense of its rightness (we affirm that it is good to be such)—of biotic communities, or the "land," as Aldo Leopold would have it, to flourish in mutual harmony. This includes human communities, of course, a vast portion of which continues, along with growing numbers of non-human species and populations, to suffer beneath the crushing weight of industrial growth society.

13. It may in fact be too late to halt the mounting wave of extinctions and long-term degradation of the biosphere. As long as there remains even a chance of avoiding the worst, however, those who can, must speak out on behalf of those most threatened, and ultimately on behalf of the entire Earth community. Arguably, the ones most qualified to speak in this way will be those who most embody, however imperfectly and provisionally, the kind of wisdom that best reflects the complex evolutionary character of Gaia, our planet-home. The trans- or meta-discipline of Big History has a vital role to play in educating such voices, a role heavy with ethical responsibility. Will it stand by, satisfied with the modernist ideal of (pseudo-)disengaged inquiry while business as usual condemns the planet to ruin, or will it strive to actualize its full potential and be an advocate for Gaia, in and through whom we have always lived and have our being?

3

Cosmological Wisdom and Planetary Madness

> *That the universe is a communion of subjects rather than a collection of objects is the central commitment of the Ecozoic.*
> —Brian Swimme and Thomas Berry

Introduction

It is a bitter irony of our times that, just as the collaborative effort of natural scientists and other researchers have revealed the outlines, at least, of a comprehensive cosmology, we should find ourselves plunged into a maelstrom of unparalleled planetary madness.[1] The madness: runaway catastrophic climate change, an accelerating mass extinction of species and generalized ecological deterioration, and a brutal, empire-driven regime of planetary apartheid. The wisdom: among the proposals for Big History type grand narratives, Swimme and Berry's *The Universe Story* (1992) that I will draw from in this chapter. It is a story that encompasses the

---

1. By "comprehensive" I mean inclusive of the known universe at all levels of organization, from the microphysical to the large-scale cosmic. Of course I recognize that various theories (the initial cosmological singularity and Big Bang, for instance) in each of the individual disciplines are contested and that there is no universally recognized overall account or "meta-theory" encompassing all of the disciplines. Nevertheless, the widespread consensus around such things as universal expansion, the history of Earth, the evolution of species, and climate change give an indication of the breadth of agreement within and among major scientific disciplines.

mysterious origin in a "primal flaring forth" (popularly referred to as the Big Bang), a growing, if perhaps never complete, understanding of the main stages of cosmic evolution, the complexities of embodied intelligence, the main thresholds of human history and the varieties of cultural expression, a sense of the lure or telos of the evolutionary adventure, and a prescient sense of growing planetary crisis.

The details of such a narrative have and continue to be provided by the assiduous efforts of countless individuals working in their respective fields of specialization. The real keepers of such narratives, however, are those (scientists or not) who dare to transgress the otherwise sensible mutual isolation of individual disciplines (and even inter- and multi-disciplines), and who are called instead, however provisionally, to articulate the nature of the Whole. In this case, the Whole includes not only the strictly physical or material-energetic dimension—whether on the large, small, or medium scale—but also the depth dimension of consciousness, interiority, meaning, and purpose. It is only when the Whole, or cosmos if one prefers, is considered in both these dimensions that the narrative becomes truly grand and a candidate, at least, for an expression of cosmological wisdom.

Cosmological

For present purposes, I focus on an expression of such wisdom that I find both economical and particularly generative—namely, Swimme and Berry's proposal for a threefold "cosmogenetic principle,"[2] or as I prefer to call it, a trinity of cosmogenetic principles. These principles—differentiation, autopoiesis (or self-organization), and communion—"refer to the governing themes and

2. B. Swimme and T. Berry, *The Universe Story: From the Primordial Flaring Forth*

the basal intentionality of all existence"[3] and can be said to reveal the deep structure of cosmogenesis. They are three mutually implicated dimensions or moments of the emergence, persistence, and evolution of form "throughout time and space and at every level of reality."[4] Swimme and Berry invoke these principles to help us understand the integral nature of cosmic evolution, from the primal flaring forth (with the mysterious relation between the original singularity—if indeed there was a singularity—and the initial break in symmetry, with its perfect, fine-tuned calibration between gravitation and the forces of expansion or spatiation and also among the four fundamental forces), through the emergence of particles, atoms, galaxies, stars (especially our own Sun), and planets (especially Earth or Gaia), to the emergence of life, human societies, and civilizations. In all cases they underline how the three principles "are themselves features of each other."[5] In fact, as they say, if were there no differentiation, "the universe would collapse into a homogenous smudge; were there no subjectivity [which Swimme and Berry associate with autopoiesis], the universe would collapse into inert, dead extension; were there no communion, the universe would collapse into isolated singularities of being."[6]

Wisdom

Swimme and Berry state that their understanding of the cosmogenetic principle is based on *post hoc* generalization from consideration of the manifest cosmos rather

---

to the Ecozoic Era—A Celebration of the Unfolding of the Cosmos (San Francisco: HarperCollins, 1992), 71.

3. Ibid.
4. Ibid.
5. Ibid., 73.
6. Ibid.

than on some a priori metaphysical (whether philosophical or theological) concept or doctrine. At the same time, however, it must be conceded that this principle is remarkably coherent with expressions of the nature of wisdom in triadic form found in the world's great metaphysical traditions.[7] We know that, before turning to scientific cosmology, Berry had undertaken a deep study of Asian traditions, particularly Neo-Confucianism. The great Neo-Confucian Zhu Xi, for instance,

> discerned a tripartite patterning or principle of the emergence of the person, and by extension, all the other objects or events of the world in terms of form or principle [*li*], dynamics or vital force [*qi*] and their unification via the mind-heart [*xin*]: the mature schematic is form, dynamics and unification. Moreover, once this unification of the principle and vital force was achieved and perfected, the outcome, at least for the human person, was a state of harmony or balance.[8]

Zhu Xi was influenced by the earlier Tiantai "original enlightenment" school of Buddhism, where we find the notion of the "threefold contemplation in one mind" (一心三観)—that is, the integral nature of the three truths of emptiness, conventional existence, and the middle. In the words of a later Japanese Tendai commentary on the threefold contemplation (*isshin sangan*):

> Everything from our own speech to the sound of the waves rising or the wind blowing is the threefold contemplation in a single mind, the originally inherent three thousand realms [i.e., all dharmas]. There is noth-

7. Kelly, *Coming Home.*

8. J.H. Berthrong, "Neo-Confucian Philosophy," *Internet Encyclopedia of Philosophy*, http://www.iep.utm.edu/neo-conf/#SH5a, (accessed September 6, 2015).

ing to cultivate and nothing to attain.... The forms of all things exerting their functions and arising in dependence upon conditions, is, without transformation, the threefold contemplation in its totality.[9]

I am not suggesting an unambiguous identification of the three cosmogenetic principles of autopoiesis, differentiation, and communion (my preferred order) with the Neo-Confucian triad of *li*, *qi*, and *xin*, or the Japanese Tendai Buddhist triad of emptiness (*kuutai*), conventional existence (*ketai*), and the middle (*chuutai*). I do believe, however, that all three triads participate in the same archetypal complex, or "cultural invariant", to use Raimon Panikkar's term, which he calls the "radical Trinity." "I may also use a consecrated name:," he writes, *"advaita* ["not twoness"], which is the equivalent of the radical Trinity. Everything is related to everything but without monistic identity or dualistic separation."[10] The most encompassing expression of the radical Trinity is the integral or non-dual "theanthropocosmic" intuition of "Reality comprising the Divine, the Human, and the Cosmic in thoroughgoing relationality."[11] "We are together with other Men," Pannikkar observes, "on a common Earth, under the same Sky, and enveloped by the Unknown."[12] These three terms remind one of the traditional Chinese triad of Heaven, Humanity, and Earth. In Panikkar's case, however, though deeply informed by both the non-dualism of Hindu *advaita vedanta* and the Buddhist notion of dependent co-arising (*pratityasamutpada*,

9. J. Stone, *Original Enlightenment and the Transformation of Medieval Japanese Buddhism* (Honolulu: University of Hawai'i Press, 1999), 178.

10. R. Panikkar, *The Rhythm of Being: The Unbroken Trinity* (Maryknoll, New York: Orbis Books, 2013), 404.

11. Ibid., xviii.

12. Ibid., 268.

which he translates as "interindependence"), the deeper source is speculative Christian Trinitarian theology (with which Berry was obviously also familiar, despite his lack of formal training in theology and his self-designation as a "geologian"). The key insight here is the "perichoretic," or mutually generating, relation among the three "persons" of the Trinity. "For Panikkar," as summarized by Rowan Williams,

> the Trinitarian structure is that of a source, inexhaustibly generative and always generative, from which arises form and determination, "being" in the sense of what can be concretely perceived and engaged with; that form itself is never exhausted, never limited by this or that specific realization, but is constantly being realized in the flux of active life that equally springs out from the source of all. Between form, "logos", and life, "spirit", there is an unceasing interaction. The Source of all does not and cannot exhaust itself simply in producing shape and structure; it also produces that which dissolves and re-forms all structures in endless and undetermined movement, in such a way that all form itself is not absolutized but always turned back toward the primal reality of the Source.[13]

Echoing Swimme and Berry's statement quoted above regarding the mutual implication of the three cosmogenetic principles, Pannikar states: "God without Man is nothing, literally 'no-thing'. Man without God is exclusively a 'thing' not a person, not a really human being, while the World, the Cosmos, without Man and God is 'any-thing' without consistency and being; it is sheer non existing chaos. The three are constitutively connected."[14]

13. Ibid., xviii.
14. R. Panikkar, *The Vedic Experience* (London: Darton, Longman & Todd, 1979),

Like Panikkar's "cosmotheanthropic" vision, Swimme and Berry see their cosmogenetic principles active throughout the entire universe story. It is in our middle realm or *Midgard* of Earth or Gaia, however, that we see the principles in action most clearly and consequentially.

Planetary

1. *autopoiesis and climate catastrophe*

The auto-poietic or self-organizing dynamics of the Earth are apparent from the time, 4.45 billion years ago, that the now cooling planet brought forth the early atmosphere, oceans, and continents, the main organs of planetary physiology. In contrast with the other planets of our solar system, Earth was graced with just the right mass, in just the right position, to allow for an exquisite dynamic balance of gravitational, nuclear, and electro-magnetic forces, allowing it to become "the advanced edge of cosmogenesis in the solar system."[15] Earth continues to be geologically very active (Mars and Venus, by contrast, are geologically frozen). This activity is not only due to its unique physical-energetic profile, however, but to the presence of life, which emerged remarkably early some 4 billion years ago. While the appearance of the first organisms can be considered as initially local emergent properties of early Gaian physiology, life quickly pervaded the oceans and began colonizing the continents, constituting a new Gaian sphere in its own right—the biosphere. As Bruce Clarke notes: "Autopoiesis and Gaia fit together as interlocking, micro- and macro- modes of systems theory: biological autopoiesis defines the minimal

73; quoted in G. Sabetta, "Panikkar's Intercultural Challenge: Philosophical, Theological and Political Aspects," https://www.academia.edu/9828052/Panik-kars_Intercultural_and_Inter-religious_Challenge (accessed August 7, 2015).

15. Swimme and Berry, *The Universe Story*, 84.

formal requirements for living systems, beginning with the cell, and Gaia captures the 'planetary physiology' of the biosphere, for which the atmosphere is the autopoietic membrane."[16]

One of the great insights of Lovelock and Margulis's Gaia theory—an insight presupposed by all subsequent Earth System science—is that the chemical composition of this membrane was established and maintained by the evolution of the biosphere, which itself depends upon the life-constituted atmosphere for its continuing existence. From the reduction of the carbon-rich early atmosphere by the prokaryotes (single cell organisms without a nucleus)—which precipitated the first ice age—through the subsequent oxygen crisis and its eventual resolution some 550 million years ago (since that time, atmospheric oxygen has stabilized between 15–35%), the biosphere "altered the terrestrial unfolding. Earth's adventure became a conversation among the hydrosphere, lithosphere, biosphere, and atmosphere."[17]

This millennial, or billennial, conversation has deteriorated in our own times, however, into a literally deadening monologue. For the first time in over 800,000 years, concentrations of atmospheric CO_2 have surpassed 400 ppm. As a result, at the time of writing, the combined average global temperature across both land surfaces and oceans has already increased by more than 1°C relative to the 20th-century average. We are already witnessing significant increases in extreme weather events (storms, floods, heat waves, unprecedented wildfires), changes in patterns of precipitation, intensifying droughts, major fluctuations in the jet stream, acidification of the oceans (which have been acting as the major carbon sink) and in-

16. B. Clarke, "Autopoiesis and the Planet."
17. Swimme and Berry, *The Universe Story*, 93.

dications of possible disruption of major ocean currents. The warming in the Arctic is three times higher than the global average. This is especially significant due to the critical role played by Acrtic ice in cooling the planet. To begin with, Acrtic ice reflects up to 90% of sunlight back into space—the so-called albedo effect. Especially given the higher level of warming, Acrtic ice is melting, decreasing the albedo, which increases the rate of warming, resulting in ice-albedo feedback. Complicating matters are the enormous stores of methane stored in both permafrost beneath the ice and in the form of hydrates in the Arctic ocean. The danger here, assuming a worst case scenario, is that

> further warming of the Arctic Ocean will unleash huge methane eruptions from the Arctic Ocean seafloor, in turn driving temperatures up even higher and causing more intense wildfires, heatwaves and further extreme weather events.... A polynomial trendline points at global temperature anomalies of over 4°C by 2060. Even worse, a polynomial trend for the Arctic shows temperature anomalies of over 4°C by 2020, 6°C by 2030 and 15°C by 2050, threatening to cause major feedbacks to kick in, including albedo changes and methane releases that will trigger runaway global warming that looks set to eventually catch up with accelerated warming in the Arctic and result in global temperature anomalies of 16°C by 2052.[18]

Even if this worst-case scenario does not pan out, the fact remains that the most recent IPCC report, which has set 2°C of warming as the upper limit beyond which we can expect irreversible catastrophic climate change (climate

18. Arctic News, http://arctic-news.blogspot.com/ (accessed August 7, 2015). For the consensus view in 2015, only slightly less alarming, see C. Mooney, "Scientists Confirm that the Arctic Could Become a Major New Source of

scientist James Hansen, by contrast, who first warned of the danger of global warming the 1980s, claims that 1°C is already catastrophic), does not factor in the feedback from the release of Arctic methane.

The literature on global warming and climate science is increasing exponentially, and there is no way I could summarize even the most relevant recent findings, projections, and analyses. While many of these are contested, and all carry a degree of uncertainty, it can be said with increasing confidence (though the word "confidence" seems emotionally out of place here) that the situation is dire. Even the most likely best-case scenarios seem to involve massive climate disruption and associated environmental catastrophe and likely civilizational collapse.

The irony of the situation, as stated in the introduction, is that the climate crisis has become the primary occasion for a growing public awareness of the self-organizing character of the Earth system. Though perhaps not conversant with the details of complex dynamical systems, more and more non-specialists understand what is meant by "tipping points" and "positive feedback". More importantly, this awareness is coupled with the realization that human beings, far from being outside observers of the "environment," are integral to the planetary system. The climate change in question is largely "anthropogenic." What this means, theoretically, is that a more adequate view of Earth or Gaia must include, alongside or interwoven with the geosphere and biosphere, an anthroposphere as its most recent epigenetic expression.

Since autopoiesis, linked as it is to systemic closure,

Carbon Emissions," *The Washington Post*, April 8, 2015. For an overview in 2020, confirming the worst case scenarios, see Julie Brigham-Grette and Steve Petsch, "The Arctic hasn't been this warm for 3 million years—and that foreshadows big changes for the rest of the planet."https://theconversation.com/the-arctic-hasnt-been-this-warm-for-3-million-years-and-that-foreshadows-big-changes-for-the-rest-of-the-planet-144544 (accessed October 25, 2020).

identity, and memory, points "to the interior dimension of things,"[19] one could say that the emergence of the anthroposphere represents the stage in the evolution of Earth where the self-organizing dynamics of Gaia bring forth, in explicit relief, the latent potential of the biosphere for self-conscious, value-driven, agency. Of course, at this point, the quality of this self-consciousness is at best fragmentary or at least functionally dissociated. Despite a growing global awareness of the threat of climate catastrophe, the overwhelming inertia of human actions and the values supporting them are in the direction of business as usual, which is to say, in support of the interests of global capitalism, in general, and of the fossil fuel industry, in particular. The dissociation is well captured in the subtitle to Naomi Klein's epochal book, *This Changes Everything: Capitalism vs. the Climate*. (Klein) "So we are left with a stark choice," she writes: "allow climate disruption to change everything about our world, or change pretty much everything about our economy to avoid that fate." [20]And not just the economy, of course, since "we need to think differently, radically differently, for those changes to be remotely possible.... For any of this to change, a worldview will need to rise to the fore that sees nature, other nations, and our own neighbors not as adversaries, but rather as partners in a grand project of mutual invention."[21]

2. *differentiation and mass extinction*
The cosmogenetic principle of differentiation manifests itself in the evolution of Earth from its inception as the variegated cloud of stellar elements that gathered to form the initial ball of molten rock (there are 92 known

19. Swimme and Berry, *The Universe Story*, 75.
20. Ibid., 22.
21. Ibid., 23.

naturally occurring elements; oxygen, iron, silicon, and magnesium account for 90% of the mass of the geosphere). The settling of core, mantle, and crust, and then the primary organs of continents, oceans, and atmosphere manifest the larger scale geophysiological differentiation (in terms of elements, the oceans are 86% oxygen and 11% hydrogen by mass, while the atmosphere is 78% nitrogen and 21% oxygen by volume). Though the early biosphere, constituted of single-cell organisms, was relatively homogenous, life would eventually differentiate into a staggering diversity of expression. It is estimated that over five billion species have emerged from the autopoietic creativity of Earth, a little more than one species for every year of its existence to date. 99% of these, however, have perished, mostly during the past five mass extinction events.

Though the news was slow in making its way into the mainstream media, it is now widely recognized that we are currently in the beginning, though accelerating, phase of the six mass extinction event.[22] The previous, Cretaceous-Paleogene mass extinction of 66 million years ago took out some three quarters of the Earth's animal and plant species, including the non-avian dinosaurs, and was likely caused by the impact of a large meteor or comet that struck the Yucatan Peninsula. The current mass extinction underway, however, is happening much faster, and it is entirely due to human activity. Like the current global climate crisis, in other words, the sixth mass extinction is anthropogenic. Though this would seem to bolster the choice of the term "Anthropocene" to describe the new geological age that humans have initiated (bringing the prior 66 million year Cenozoic to a close),

---

22. Ceballos et al. represents the most recent, conservative estimate of 100 times the background extinction rate; for the more likely rate of 1000 times, see Pimm et al.

the fact that humans are also on the potential extinction list should cast considerable doubt, or at least irony, on this choice of terms. While it is true that the previous mass extinctions made way for new waves of specia-tion—diversification through annihilation, one could say—it is quite possible that the striking exfoliations of life following the Permian and Cretaceous extinctions were Gaia's last great gestures of biological exuberance. In any case, since it has taken many millions of years for the biosphere to recover from past extinctions, and since the average life span of mammalian species is one million years, it is highly unlikely that humans will be around to enjoy what other life forms manage to survive.

The major drivers of the current mass extinction include habitat loss (especially forests and wetlands), ecological degradation (including monocultures, invasive species, pollution), species exploitation (over-fishing, hunting), ocean acidification (a special case of pollution), and of course global warming. Global warming not only exacerbates the other drivers, but is coupled with them, and especially habitat loss and ecological degradation, in a death-dealing positive feedback loop. The main driv-er, however, is the activity of the anthroposphere itself, whose global footprint, under the capitalist regime of industrial growth society, is currently at one and a half Earths and projected to be at three Earths by 2050 (that is, it would take three Earths to provide the resources consumed and to absorb the wastes produced).[23] Of course, there is only one Earth, and most of what will be consumed or lost (fossil fuels, the remaining old growth forests, countless species) can never be replaced. As far as the current mass extinction and global warming are concerned (and the two, as I have said, are coupled in a

23. See *Global Footprint Network*, http://www.footprintnetwork.org/en/index. php/GFN/page/world_footprint/ (accessed April 25, 2020).

mutually amplifying feedback loop), we seem to have a very short window—a decade at most—to turn things around and avoid the worst case scenario.

Though perhaps initially counterintuitive, the assault on Gaian biodiversity can be understood as the result of a hypertrophy of the principle of differentiation in the anthroposphere. A distinguishing character of the human is the ability to order its experience and its world through the mediation of symbols. Though symbolic consciousness is naturally associated primarily with language, it is present wherever categorial distinctions are in play. In social contexts, for instance, one finds the primal distinction between insider and outsider, divisions of labor, levels of status or privilege, and so on. In terms of the current planetary crisis, we could point to three related paradigmatic or meta-level expressions of hypertrophic differentiation. The first is patriarchy, which has dominated socio-cultural evolution throughout the historical period. Feminist scholars have demonstrated the intrinsic alliance between the subordination of women and women's value spheres, on the one hand, and the domination of nature or the material realm in general, on the other.[24] As for the domination of nature, while it is true that humans have spoiled, denuded, or otherwise disrupted their natural environments for many thousands of years, it was not until the advent of modern science and technology—the second expression of hypertrophic differentiation—and particularly following the industrial revolution and the exploitation of fossil fuels, that humans became ecocidal on a planetary scale. The modern scientific par-

24. See C. Merchant, *The Death of Nature: Women, Ecology and the Scientific Revolution* (San Francisco: HarperOne, 1990); C. Spretnak, *States of Grace: The Recovery of Meaning in the Postmodern Age* (San Francisco: Harper San Francisco, 1993); C. Keller, *From a Broken Web: Separation, Sexism, and Self* (Boston: Beacon Press, 1988).

adigm is founded on the root metaphor of the cosmos as machine, the constitutive elements of which are thought of as lifeless and merely externally related to one another. Scientific knowledge is primarily instrumental, allowing for the prediction and control of objects for human use.

Again, however, even patriarchy and modern science and technology would not, by themselves, be able to lead the planet to the edge of catastrophe were it not for the third expression of hypertrophic differentiation—namely, global capitalism. Making full use of the other-dominating, instrumentalist attitudes and practices of the first two expressions, capitalism, to begin with in alliance with colonialism and then also in the form of corporatocracy, quickly became its own planet-wide autopoietic force. While it is the case that the universe story and the Gaian consciousness that it celebrates would not have emerged without this world-making force, its creative role is now overshadowed by its apocalyptic potential.

3. communion and Empire

Like the third moment in the Hegelian dialectic, or the Holy Spirit of the Christian Trinity, the third cosmogenetic principle—communion—is simultaneously presupposed by the first two, and the expression of their harmonious interplay. It is presupposed because there can be neither self-making nor differentiation without real internal and external relations. At the same time, true communion is impossible between essentially lifeless (no identity) or completely identical (no difference) entities. It is only with the full expression of communion, therefore, that the creative potential of the cosmogenetic principle can be fully actualized. "The universe," write Swimme and Berry, "evolves into beings that are different from each other, and that organize themselves. But in addition to this, the universe advances into community—

into a differentiated web of relationships among sentient beings."[25] The principle of communion is evident at all scales of the cosmos and at all stages of the evolutionary journey: in the quantum entanglement of elementary particles; in the mutual gravitational attraction of galaxies, stars, and planets; in the miraculous origin of life in the prolonged courtship of organic molecules and lightning in the primordial oceans; in the symbiogenetic mergers that birthed the first eukaryotic cells; in the complex webs of ecosystem communication; in the millions of years of mammalian bondings; in the forgotten gatherings of archaic hominid societies; in the many histories, mostly unwritten, of creative human collaboration, mutual assistance, and celebration.

"The loss of relationship," by contrast, "with its consequent alienation, is a kind of supreme evil in the universe.... To be locked up in a private world, to be cut off from intimacy with other beings, to be incapable of entering the joy of mutual presence—such conditions were taken [in traditional religious contexts] as the essence of damnation."[26] While every living being will, at one time or another, experience moments of alienation, and while human history is in no small measure a history of oppression, our own times are the first to be organized on the basis of systematic alienation on a planetary scale. Granting such remarkable achievements as the abolition of slavery, women's suffrage, and a widespread affirmation, in principle at least, of the ideal of universal human rights, it is nevertheless the case that approximately half the world population lives in extreme poverty and the deprivations with which it is associated. Thomas Pogge sums up the situation as follows:

25. Swimme and Berry, *The Universe Story*, 77.
26. Ibid., 78.

The collective income of all these people—the bottom half—is less than three percent of global household income, and so there is a grotesque maldistribution of income and wealth. The bottom quarter of the human population has only three-quarters of one percent of global household income, about one thirty-second of the average income in the world, whereas the people in the top five percent have nine times the average income. So the ratio between the averages in the top five percent and the bottom quarter is somewhere around 300 to one....[27]

The statistics on global wealth inequality are even more obscene, with the wealthiest 1% owning more than the remaining 99%.[28] Measures of relative wealth and poverty are perhaps the single most revealing indicators of the full range of inequalities, beginning with access to—or quality of—food, water, and shelter, and including access to education, social services, and other factors contributing to quality of life.

As it now stands, the world situation can be described as a kind of planetary apartheid. I use the word planetary instead of global here so as to include other than human beings in the equation, the larger portion of whom, as we have seen above, are on the verge of extinction.[29] Along with the billions of humans living in misery, there are 10 billion animals (approximately 1.3 for every human being on the planet) reared in concentration camps (factory

27.   T. Pogge and K. Bhatt, "Thomas Pogge on the Past, Present and Future of Global Poverty," *Truthout*, May 29, 2011, http://www.truth-out.org/news/item/792:thomas-pogge-on-the-past-present-and-future-of-global-poverty (accessed August 2, 2015).

28.   See L. Elliot and E. Pilkington, "New Oxfam Report Says Half of Global Wealth Held by the 1%," *The Guardian*, January 19, 2015, http://www.theguardian.com/business/2015/jan/19/global-wealth-oxfam-inequality-davos-economic-summit-switzerland (accessed August 2, 2015).

29.   For the meaning of the term global apartheid, see Mutassa.

farms) each year for human use. The two classes of oppressed—human and other than human—are the victims of a single overarching system or regime, which can perhaps best be described with the term Empire. In David Korten's formulation, Empire is based on

> the hierarchical ordering of human relationships [among humans and between humans and other than humans] based on the principle of domination. The mentality of Empire embraces material excess for the ruling classes, honors the dominator power of death and violence, denies the feminine principle, and suppresses the realization of the potentials of human [and other than human] maturity.[30]

Unlike smaller empires throughout the historical period, the current global Empire does not have a single standing army to impose its rule. While the military industrial complex, or complexes, together constitute a significant player in the global economy, the rule of Empire is maintained through the pervasive power of global capitalism—which is to say, the private ownership (overwhelmingly by the 1%) of the forces of production. The latter include the various industries, the goods produced (whether material or informational), and the labor used to produce them, along with mechanisms not only to profit through the trading of financial capital, but the power literally to create money out of thin air (fiat currency). Marx was the first to articulate the ways in which individuals and classes are alienated under capitalist modes of production—alienated from the products of their labor, from the process of production, from other people, from the natural world.

---

30. D. Korten, *The Great Turning: From Empire to Earth Community* (Bloomfield: Kumarian Press, 2006), 20.

There are three mutually enabling features of capitalism—an unholy trinity, if you will—that I would underline here, which I could describe in terms of motive, means, and mode. The main motive is cupidity or greed for gain, which takes the form of the pursuit of maximization of profit and continuous growth in revenues. This is achieved by various means, but must ultimately rely on the discovery or creation of new markets, cheap labor, the disposability or obsolescence of products, and the stimulation of desire for new products. As has now become obvious, the successful pursuit of continuous growth has also relied on the assumption of infinite resources (material and energetic) and the so-called externalization of costs to both human societies and the natural environment. The latter form of externalization, which amounts to a degradation of natural systems, exacerbates the effects of resource depletion through over-exploitation (for instance, ocean acidification from CO_2 pollution amplifying collapse of marine species through over-fishing).

The means by which global capitalism achieves its motive is the private ownership of what would otherwise be—and arguably, what ought to be—owned in common. As long as one could ignore externalization of costs, it is at least understandable how people could be blind to the injustice of private ownership of productive forces. Unless one is persuaded, as I am, by the Marxist ethical analysis of how profit depends on alienated labor—on a form of theft, in other words—it might not be evident why, for instance, a creative and hard-working entrepreneur should not be able to own his own business—say, a chain of grocery stores that caters to educated, environmentally conscious consumers—especially if his employees are all paid above the minimum wage.

Where the wrong of private ownership of the commons (including labor) becomes glaringly obvious is when the nature of productive activity is set in its full ecological context—that is, in the planetary or Gaian commons in which we live and have our being. In this context, there can be no "externalization" of costs. This realization first came to public awareness with the cross-border effects of acid rain, but of course is now fully apparent and calling for decisive action in connection with the catastrophic effects of atmospheric CO_2 generated by capitalist industries. Though less obvious, the same concern ought to be extended to the presence and continued release of radio-nucleotides, persistent organic chemicals, and other toxins into the biosphere. The presence of all such toxins, including CO_2, though suffered by every living thing on the planet (and more immediately and intensely by the socio-economically disadvantaged), are the result of capitalist modes of production, and thus flow from the decisions of the 1% (who also reap most of the benefit). The same is true, of course, for the generalized degradation of the biosphere (habitat loss, decimation of plant and animal species through over-exploitation, industrial mono-cropping, etc.). The point, therefore, is that the greed-guided, private ownership of productive forces that constitutes capitalism is incompatible—in both real and ethical terms—with the fact of the planetary commons.[31]

The mode of global capitalism, or of Empire, can be described in terms of the root paradigmatic assumption of the dominant late-modern worldview. The latter has been characterized variously as mechanistic, techno-centric

---

31. I know that many will say that the problem is not capitalism as such, but "predatory" or "unregulated" capitalism. If I am correct in my view of the motive, means, and mode of capitalism, however, capitalism is "predatory" by nature, which is why, if it is to exist at all, it needs to be heavily regulated! In this connection, see D. Graeber, "Savage Capitalism is Back – and It will not Tame Itself," *The Guardian*, May 30, 2014, http://www.theguardian.com/commentis-free/2014/may/30/savage-capitalism-back-radical-challenge?CMP=share_btn_fb (accessed September 21, 2015).

or technocratic, reductionistic, instrumentalist, rational-
istic, economistic, and disenchanted. All of these terms
presuppose a view of the universe as a "collection of
objects"[32]—that is, as essentially inert things with merely
extrinsic value (which, in the capitalist system, is defined in terms of commodities). Regardless of where one
might stand, given their autopoietic nature, with respect
to the subjectivity of fundamental particles, atoms, stars
and galaxies, or even of the simpler organisms, it is now
almost universally recognized that human beings are not
objects to be bought or sold (this despite the persistence
of human trafficking, and both wage and debt slavery).
Because of the ecological solidarity of human beings
with the Gaian system, however—a solidarity which
means that Earth is not merely our environment, but
in a very real sense our extended body, which, through
rampant privatization of the commons, *is* being bought
and sold—we are brought once again to the fundamental contradiction of capitalism, again, well captured by
the subtitle of Klein's book, *This Changes Everything:
Capitalism vs. the Climate*, and the subtitle of Korten's
earlier, more comprehensive work, *The Great Turning:
From Empire to Earth Community*.

As an indication of the supraordinate character of the
principle of communion, Swimme and Berry make the
following claim: "That the universe is a communion of
subjects rather than a collection of objects is the central
commitment of the Ecozoic."[33] The term Ecozoic is their
proposal for the geological age in process of succeeding
the 66 million year Cenozoic. "The comprehensive objective of the Ecozoic," they affirm,

32. Swimme and Berry, *The Universe Story*, 243.
33. Ibid.

is to assist in establishing a mutually enhancing human presence on the Earth.... The immediate goal... is not simply to diminish the devastation of the planet that is taking place at present. It is rather to alter the consciousness that is responsible for such deadly activities.[34]

Swimme and Berry speak of the need to evoke a "counter to the commercial-industrial mystique"[35] that has "misenchanted" (Segall) the modern mind. Overriding traditional political and ideological divisions, they assert that

the dominant issue of the immediate future will be the tension between the Entrepreneur and the Ecologist, between those who would continue their plundering, and those who would truly preserve the natural world, between the mechanistic and the organic, between the world as collection of objects and the world as a communion of subjects, between the anthropocentric and the biocentric norms of reality and value.[36]

Conclusion:
homo sapiens-demens and the Gaianthropocene

Though I agree with its spirit, I would amend the terms of the last opposition in the passage just quoted. It is certainly the case that the human presence on the planet has become ecocidal. To my mind, however, the root problem is not so much anthropocentrism per se as a mutilated understanding of anthropos, where the human has set itself, in deed if not in theory, above or outside of the cosmological reality in which it is in fact embedded. At the same time, however, it is equally

34. Ibid., 250–51.
35. Ibid., 250.
36. Ibid.

true that this cosmological reality is only given to us as mediated through our specifically human life-world. It is, after all, human science and reflection that have brought forth the universe story. Practically speaking, moreover, it is the case, as Swimme and Berry themselves recognize, that if "the emergence of the Cenozoic in all its brilliance was independent of any human influence, almost every phase of the Ecozoic will involve the human. While the human cannot make a blade of grass, there is liable not to be a blade of grass unless it is accepted, protected, and fostered by the human."[37] It is for these reasons that there is a virtual consensus around the term Anthropocene to describe the dawning geological era. The danger of this term, however, is that it will amplify the hubris in the dominant, mutilated and myopic understanding of the human as preeminently *homo faber, technologicus,* or *economicus.*

As for the self-designation of humans as *homo sapiens sapiens,* the lone survivor among the genus *homo,* one might understandably question the unqualified attribution of the term "wise", let alone its doubling (the "wisest among the wise"). We have, it is true, the undisputed brilliance of human intelligence as seen not only in our own times with the grand, if still and perhaps forever incomplete narrative of the universe story, and more generally in the awesome variety of human cultural expression (in art, religion, and philosophy; in the human and social sciences generally; in the myriad traditions of indigenous knowledge and practice). At the same time, the human story has also been one of violence and bigotry, of superstition and illusion, and at least throughout the historical period, of domination through war, slavery, dispossession, and persecution. In the last

---

37. Ibid., 247.

century, the destructive potential of our species reached planetary proportions with the first world wars and the three symptoms of planetary madness that I have focused on in these pages: climate catastrophe, mass extinction of species, and planetary apartheid. Given this shadow that has always accompanied the light in which we would like to behold ourselves, a more apt term for our species, as Edgar Morin has proposed, would be *homo sapiens-demens*, the "wise-mad" animal.

This potential for madness, however, is not limited to the aggression of the Freudian death instinct (*thanatos*). The *demens* in question, though it can and has expressed itself demonically, is also the source of the *daimonic*— that is, the imaginal, inspirational, ecstatic, and participatory modes of being in the world. The attempt to banish the daimonic is its own form of madness, a dissociation of that which is, or should be, complexly interwoven. "The bipolarity of *sapiens-demens*," writes Morin,

> is the extreme expression of the existential bipolarity of the two kinds of life which weave our lives, one serious, utilitarian, and prosaic, the other playful, aesthetic, poetic.... Moreover, *sapiens* is within *demens* and *demens* is within *sapiens*, as with the yin and yang, each one containing the other. Between one and the other, in a manner both antagonistic and complementary, there is no clear boundary.... A totally rational, technical, and utilitarian life would not only be demented, but inconceivable. A life without any kind of rationality would be equally impossible...
>
> Human beings live not only through rationality and tools; they make use of and give themselves over to dance, trance, myth, magic, and ritual.... Play, celebration, rituals, are not simply forms of relaxation that allow one to return to the practical life of work. Belief in gods and ideas cannot be reduced to the status of

illusion or superstition: they have roots that plunge into the depths of human nature.... This is the paradox, the richness, the prodigality, the discontent, the happiness of *homo sapiens-demens*.[38]

Acknowledging the truth of what is suggested by the term Anthropocene, though affirming the ideal of the Ecozoic as conceived by Swimme and Berry, the new era that we have initiated might best be described by the term *Gaianthropocene*. Like the bipolarity of *homo sapiens-demens*, the advantage of this term is that it suggests the complex character of the relation between humans and Earth. Complex because the nature and destiny of each term is interwoven with the other (*com-plexere*, to weave together). Though there was once an Earth without humans, there will no longer be an Earth without the presence of the human. Even after the passing of the last of our species, whether through self-induced extinction or through the inevitable demise of what remains of the biosphere (at the limit, when, in 3 billion years, the oceans begin to boil off from steadily increasing solar radiation), Earth's geochemistry, if nothing else, will still carry the signature of our world-transforming activities (for instance, to mention just one example, with the global presence and distribution of anthropogenic depleted uranium, whose half-life is over 4.5 billion years).

The relation between Gaia and anthropos is also complex (in Morin's understanding of complexity) in that it is dialogical, recursive, holographic, and uncertain.[39] It is dialogical because human being is both complementary

---

38. E. Morin, *La Méthode 5: L'Identité Humaine* (Paris: Éditions du Seuil, 2001), 131.

39. For an extended discussion of Morin's "paradigm of complexity," see S. Kelly, "Integral Ecology and Edgar Morin's Paradigm of Complexity," in *The Variety of Integral Ecologies: Nature, Culture, and Knowledge in the Planetary Era*, eds. Sam Mickey, Sean Kelly, and Adam Robbert (Albany: SUNY, 2017).

(as a potentially synergistic partner) and antagonistic (to the point of ecocide) relative to the wider Gaian system. It is recursive in that, though an emergent product of Gaian evolution, the human has itself become a significant causal factor in this evolution. It is holographic insofar as each term, in important ways, both contains and is contained by the other (that humans are part of the encompassing whole that is Gaia should be obvious. That Gaia is contained by the human is most apparent with the idea and fact of the anthroposphere, the outermost though, as we have seen, now most consequential layer of the Gaian system).

Finally, the relation is uncertain, not only relative to the ultimate ground and details of their respective origins and entwined histories, but also in their ultimate fates. While there is a relatively solid consensus around the likely demise of the planet in cosmological terms (a maximum life expectancy of another 3 or 4 billion years), in the near to middle term, at least, there is an unknown set of possible alternative futures. With each month and year that passes, however, a future that includes the kind of magnificent biodiversity that preceded and has always supported our species, if indeed a real possibility, becomes less and less probable. As the web of life itself continues to unravel, so too will the recently woven fabric of planetary civilization. We do not yet know, though surely some alive today will know, if we can halt our hurtling ever deeper into planetary madness. At the very least, we know what is at stake and what must be done to have a fighting chance of avoiding the worst.

4

Sources of the Good: A Complex-Integral Ethic for the Planetary Era

Never before in the history of humanity have the responsibilities of thinking weighed so crushingly on us.
—Edgar Morin

Introduction

In one form or another and to varying degrees, the burden of ethical choices has doubtless weighed on human consciousness from its inception. In the last few years, however, the burden has tipped all previous scales as the consequences of our actions take on the weight of the planet itself, or at least that of the wider Earth community, whose fate now lies largely in our hands. Or perhaps our minds or consciousness as much as our hands, since our actions are expressions of mental, psychic, and spiritual choices. These choices started assuming planetary proportions about five hundred years ago when, through the voyages of conquest and discovery, humans first circumnavigated the globe, establishing stable and continuous intercontinental exchanges and communications.[1] This was followed soon after by the Copernican revolution, which revealed that the Earth is indeed a planet, a "wanderer" like the other planets, and not the static center of the medieval universe. Over the

---

1. See Kelly, *Coming Home.*

next few centuries, the modern scientific, industrial, and political revolutions would deconstruct and disenchant this universe. The project of modernity has liberated nations, raised the quality of life for billions of people and has birthed scientific and technological wonders. At the same time, as we saw in the previous chapter, modern industrial growth society has created a state of planetary apartheid with incalculable human suffering, has initiated a mass extinction of species and brought the biosphere itself to the brink of collapse. Though the Planetary Era began five centuries ago, by all reasonable accounts, we now have a decade at most to make the right choices for there to be even a chance of avoiding what seems like an inevitable planetary catastrophe. The nature of the Planetary Era, therefore, if not explicitly in its beginnings, now reveals itself as ethical to the core.

"Never before in the history of humanity," writes Morin, "have the responsibilities of thinking weighed so crushingly on us."[2] "Thinking" here includes all forms of meaning attribution and creation, whether conscious or not, conceptual or symbolic, individual or collective. Clearly, since all of our actions and their consequences are guided by and suffused with such meaning, there is a critical role for theory which is able to assume a meta-point of view relative to all forms of thinking, broadly conceived. Such is the case with the project of integral theory pioneered by Ken Wilber and the method (or "Way") of complexity initiated by Edgar Morin, both of which, along with the ecozoic vision of Thomas Berry (and Brian Swimme) considered in the previous chapter, are foundational to the emerging field of integral ecologies[3]. In what follows, I highlight the distinctive virtues

2. Morin with Kerne, Homeland Earth, 132.
3. See S. Mickey, S. Kelly, and A. Robbert, eds., *The Variety of Integral Ecologies: Nature, Culture, and Knowledge in the Planetary Era* (Albany: SUNY Press, 2017).

(and possible shortcomings) of Wilber's and Morin's respective approaches, a dialogical encounter between which opens the way for a "complex-integral" mode of theorizing and a corresponding complex-integral ethic that might assist us in becoming more responsible participants in this most critical phase of the Planetary Era.

According to Morin, our sense of the ethical inhabits, or emerges from, three primary sites, which are therefore three sources of the good: the individual, society, and the species. While all of these terms are complex, the last two are also ambiguous in Morin's use of them. By society, Morin sometimes includes culture. Instead of species, he sometimes refers to the more general and inclusive terms of human nature, the "anthropological," or to the cosmos or universe, and especially in the form of life, in which the human is embedded. Ethical imperatives, he writes,

> have their source within the individual, who possesses a mental or spiritual sense of moral injunction. But they also have external sources: the culture, beliefs, and norms of a community. There is doubtless a prior source in living organization itself which is transmitted genetically.[4]
>
> ...
>
> There is no question of establishing a foundation for the ethical, but rather of re-sourcing and regenerating it in the loop of re-liance:
>
> individual → species → society[5]

"Might there not also be," he also wonders, "beneath this anthropological layer, a quasi-primordial re-sourcing

4. E. Morin, *La Méthode 6: Éthique* (Paris: Éditions du Seuil, 2004), 13. All translations of Morin are my own.

5. Ibid., 26.

and re-liance that puts us in touch with the fifteen-billion year distant origin of the universe itself?"[6] I shall have more to say about this mysterious origin and the crucial concept of re-liance later.

As for these three sources, readers of Wilber will immediately recognize in them his corresponding notion of the "Big Three" of "I, We, and It," which he correlates with the realms of subjectivity, inter-subjectivity, and objectivity, respectively. Drawing on the thought of Max Weber, Jurgen Habermas, and Charles Taylor, among others, Wilber characterizes the main achievement and "dignity" of modernity as having to do with the differentiation of the Big Three. The differentiation of nature (It) from the preconceptions of ancient and medieval theology and the authority of the Church (We), for instance, allowed for the emergence of modern science. Similarly, the differentiation of individual consciousness and conscience (I) from the authority of church, monarchy, and state (We) led to the eventual declaration of universal human rights and to the various "liberation movements from abolition to feminism."[7] According to Wilber, however, the late modern period, dominated by the mechanistic "Enlightenment paradigm," has seen this differentiation pass over into a pathological dissociation. And with this dissociation, the "great nightmare of scientific materialism was upon us (Whitehead), the nightmare of one-dimensional man (Marcuse), the disqualified universe (Mumford), the colonization of art and morals by science (Habermas), the disenchantment of the world (Weber)—a nightmare I have also called flatland."[8] Such is the "disaster" of late modernity.

6. Ibid.

7. K. Wilber, *Integral Psychology: Consciousness, Spirit, Psychology, Therapy* (London: Shambhala 2000), 69.

8. Ibid., 70.

Focusing on the ethical implications of the late modern dissociation among the terms of his own version of the Big Three, Morin notes that the traditional sources of the good have dried up:

> the source in the individual is asphyxiated by egocentrism; the communal source is dehydrated by the degradation of solidarities; the social is distorted by the compartmentalization, bureaucratization, and atomization of social life...; the bio-anthropological source is weakened by the primacy of the individual over the species.
>
> The development of individualism leads to nihilism...: the anxiety associated with the nostalgia for a lost sense of community, of foundations, of the meaning of life, can entail a return to former national, ethnic and/or religious communal foundations accompanied by a sense of psychological security and ethical support.[9]

Though he has not developed an explicit or systematic evolutionary framework in his writings, Morin clearly presupposes the fundamental three-phase structure found in Wilber (and Hegel, Jung, Gebser, and so many others).[10] The shift from the first to the second phase, which coincides with the birth of the Planetary Era, is marked by the differentiation of the Big Three (with the first phase represented by their relative fusion). As we have just seen, however, this differentiation has passed over into dissociation ("egocentrism," "compartmentalization," "atomization" etc.), which has spawned compensatory regressions (most notably with the rise of malignant fundamentalisms). The third phase involves the (re) integration of the Big Three.

9. Morin, *La Méthode 6*, 24.
10. See Kelly, *Coming Home*.

Before turning to the specifics of this third phase, however, I want to consider a few details of our "nightmare" moment in the second. The particular structure and stage in play in Wilber's model is that of the rational-egoic or late-mental. There is nothing intrinsically pathological about this stage or the rational or mental structure in general. In fact, there can be no fully actualized ethical consciousness without it, even if, as we shall see, the kind of formal-operational thinking associated with this structure, though necessary, is not sufficient for such consciousness. As part of the "fundamental Enlightenment paradigm," however, the mental structure becomes "deficient," as Gebser puts it,[11] which we recognize in the colonization of all aspects of life by what Morin calls the "logic of the artificial machine." "The extension of the logic of the artificial machine to every aspect of life," Morin notes, "produces mechanistic and fragmented thinking that takes technocratic and econocratic form..."[12] While this logic is relatively autonomous,[13] it is also clearly in the service of the world's power elite. The exponential curve of technological advance, for instance, as we saw in the previous chapter, is not only matched but also driven by the pursuit of the maximization of profit that guides the global capitalist system.

In other words, while individuals (I) may be atomized and alienated under the pervasive influence of deficient mental culture, they nevertheless remain in specific kinds of relationship with other individuals (We) and with the environment in general (It). We certainly gain insight into the character of these relationships by recognizing the

11. Gebser, *The Ever-present Origin*.

12. Morin with Kerne, *Homeland Earth*, 70.

13. In this connection, see Jacques Ellul's understanding of the self-perpetuating reign of technique. J. Ellul, *The Technological Society* (New York: Vintage Books, 1954).

role of the deficient mental in the fundamental Enlightenment paradigm and the instrumental logic of the artificial
machine. The properly ethical dimension, however, only
becomes explicit with the recognition that this logic, this
paradigm serves to bolster and perpetuate a series of related power asymmetries: human over nature, "developed"
over "underdeveloped" or "developing"; men over wom-
en; white over colored, etc. Morin makes this connection
when he writes that,

> [a]fter thirty years devoted to development, the great
> North/South imbalance remains, and inequalities are
> worsening. Twenty five percent of the world's popula-
> tion, living in the rich countries, consumes seventy-five
> percent of the energy. The great powers retain a monop-
> oly on high technology and even possess a cognitive and
> manipulative power over the genetic material of living
> species, including the human.... The Third World contin-
> ues to suffer economic exploitation from the developed
> world, but also from its blindness, closed-mindedness,
> and moral and intellectual underdevelopment.[14]

Though he tends, like Morin, to emphasize the
more pervasive and systemic dissociative character of
the deficient mental phase of consciousness, in an earlier
work,[15] Wilber explores the helpful notion of "relational exchange" which allows us to see how "each level of
the compound human individual is exercised in a complex system of ideally unobstructed exchanges with the
corresponding levels of the world process at large."[16] In
fact, however, the historical period has yet to achieve

---

14. Morin with Kerne, *Homeland Earth*, 60.
15. K. Wilber, *Up from Eden: A Transpersonal View of Human Evolution*, in *The Collected Works of Ken Wilber, Volume Two* (Boston: Shambhala, 1999).
16. Ibid., 582.

the ideal and has instead been characterized by various kinds of "exchange distortion" involving both (external) oppression and (internal) repression. The levels (and some typically associated distortions) in question are, in ascending order: material (slavery, alienated labor, appropriation of the commons), sexual-emotional (sexual and emotional abuse, sexism), verbal-symbolic (racism, cultural chauvinism, sexism in discourse), and mental-egoic (self-deception, shadow projection). On the "dignity" side of the ledger, the differentiation of the mental-ego, especially following the modern differentiation of the Big Three, has brought in its train not only the liberating potentials of critical, formal operational thinking and self-reflexivity, but also exchanges of mutual recognition and self-esteem upon which ethical culture depends. These exchanges, Wilber admits, "might not have been universally implemented and respected, but the *potential* for such exchanges was clearly present."[17]

On the "disaster" side of the ledger, the superior power of the mental-ego—especially in its deficient mode—"resulted in the *possibility* (not necessity) of even more brutal terrors exercised *by* the ego";

> new substitute sacrifices, mass homicide, oppressive exploitation, massive slavery, ecological despoliation, class alienation, violent inequality, hedonistic overindulgence, and wildly exaggerated substitute gratifications—all of which could cripple the levels of exchange both in oneself and in the others who happened to fall under one's influence or power.[18]

Clearly, then, to grasp the full ethical import of the pathological manifestation of the second main phase in

17. Ibid., 607.
18. Ibid., 608.

the evolution of consciousness, one must recognize not only the dissociation of the Big Three, but more specifically the cancer of oppressive/exploitative and repressive regimes within each of, and between, the I, the We, and It, or in Morin's formulation, the individual, society, and species (or better, as we shall see later, the wider Earth community).

THE INDIVIDUAL

The transition to the third, complex-integral phase of the evolution of consciousness will involve a radical reorganization of each of the Big Three and the relations among them. Wilber and Morin both agree, however, that the transformation of the I, or individual consciousness, must lead the transition. It is true that individual consciousness does not exist in isolation, that it is co-constituted by the body and by its social and cultural relations, as these in turn are co-constituted by the individual (more on this below). From the ethical perspective, however, it is individual consciousness that leads, since it is only here that there is the possibility of choice and responsible agency. "The individual," writes Morin, "is irreducible."

> All attempts to reduce [the individual] to the species or to society are misguided. The human individual... possesses the attributes of mind or spirit: it is superior to the species and to society because it alone possesses a conscience and the fullness of subjectivity. The possibility of individual autonomy is actualized through the historical emergence of individualism, all the while remaining inseparable from the fate of historical and social processes.
>
> Thus, the individual is neither alpha nor omega, but the Gordian knot of the human trinity.[19]

19. Morin, *La Méthode* 5, 63–64.

The transformation of the I or individual in the development of ethical consciousness involves a progressive
widening and deepening of self-identity and its capacity
for empathic embrace. As with the evolution of consciousness in general, in ethical development there are
three broad phases: preconventional, conventional, and
postconventional. The first phase is associated with
two main perspectives or worldviews: egocentric (the
seemingly isolated individual) and ethnocentric (family,
tribe). The second phase is largely sociocentric (ethnicity,
nation). The third, postconventional phase is minimally
worldcentric or planetary, though Wilber recognizes the
possibility of further, "post-postconventional" stages
of development which he characterizes as theocentric
(which itself has at least three sub-phases).

The transition to a worldcentric or planetary ethical
perspective requires that the individual be able to enact
the rudiments, at least, of what Wilber calls "vision-logic"—which, he claims, "underlies the possibility of a
truly planetary culture (or, rather, the first true forms of
planetary organization...)"[20]—and of what Morin calls
complex thinking. As for vision-logic, Wilber writes that
it "can hold in mind contradictions, it can unify oppo-
sites, it is dialectical and non-linear, and it weaves together what otherwise appears as incompatible notions, as
long as they relate together in the new and higher holon,
negated in their partiality but preserved in their positive
contributions..."[21] This is very close to Morin's characterization of the need for complex thinking when faced with
"the irruption of antagonisms at the heart of organized
phenomena" and of "paradoxes or contradictions at the
heart of theories." As with vision-logic, complex thinking

20. K. Wilber, *Sex, Ecology, Spirituality, in The Collected Works of Ken Wilber,
Volume Six* (Boston: Shambhala, 2000), 191.
21. Ibid.

involves the task of holding together, without inco-
herence, two (or more) ideas which are nonetheless
contrary to one another. This is not possible unless we
find, a) the meta-point of view that relativizes contradiction, and b) a way to insert into a productive
feedback loop antagonistic concepts which thereby also
become complementary.[22]

There is no guarantee, of course, that such thinking will
necessarily translate into a worldcentric or planetary ethic. There must surely be sociopaths, for instance, capable
of such thinking who are simultaneously incapable of
truly *feeling into* other perspectives, of actually empa-
thizing with others.[23] Vision-logic or complex thinking,
therefore, is not sufficient, though it may be necessary,
for the transformation of the individual and the corresponding transition into a genuinely postconventional,
worldcentric ethical (meta)perspective.

In this connection, Wilber has noted that "research
continues to suggest that cognitive development is necessary but not sufficient for interpersonal development,
which is necessary but not sufficient for moral development, which is necessary but not sufficient for ideas of
the Good."[24] Though we may consider moral or ethical
development, as Wilber does, in terms of a relatively independent line, it might be more helpful to think in terms
of a fabric instead. An ethical perspective would be more

22. E. Morin, *La Méthode 1: La Nature de la Nature* (Paris: Éditions du Seuil,
1977), 379.

23. I note in passing here that many transnational corporations, though enjoy-
ing the legal status of persons, and despite their planetary scope, are involved in
the perpetuation of global apartheid and possible ecocide, and thus are far from
embodying a worldcentric ethical perspective. Presumably the same is true of
many of their board members and strategists, at least when thinking/feeling on
behalf of their corporations.

24. Wilber, *Integral Psychology*, 46.

or less supple, resilient, useful, true, and even beautiful, depending upon which and how the various strands or lines are woven or folded together (*com-plexere*). Since we know that a postconventional ethical perspective demands that the individual be able not only to think, but also to *feel*, the position of the other(s), we can assume that a viable ethical fabric must consist of at least the cognitive and affective lines. In stronger terms, we could say that cognition itself, at every stage of development, is also a kind of fabric. Our judgments as to the *what* of things is never a matter of purely conceptual determinations. "We now know," writes Morin, "that every rational act of the mind is accompanied by affect. Though it can immobilize reason, only affect is capable of mobilizing it."[25] As the work of Antonio Damasio[26] and other neuroscientists have demonstrated,[27] many dimensions of cognition are intimately associated with (usually unconscious) emotional responses. Add to this the insights of Gerald Holton[28] into the role of "themata" in scientific theory (such as the preference for simplicity, or the conviction that matter is decomposable into ultimately, indivisible elements) or those of Jung and Pauli on the role of archetypal intuitions in science,[29] and we start to discern the multiplicity of strands woven into even the most abstract, formal-operational cognition.

Still, we can, with caution, speak heuristically of the cognitive and emotional (and interpersonal and esthet-

25. Morin, *La Méthode: 6*, 152.

26. A. Damasio, *The Feeling of What Happens: Body and Emotion in the Making of Consciousness* (Boston: Mariner Books, 2000).

27. See L. Pessoa, "Cognition and Emotion," Scholarpedia, doi:10.4249/scholarpedia.4567 (accessed May 2, 2020).

28. G.J. Holton, *Thematic Origins of Scientific Thought: Kepler to Einstein* (Cambridge, MA: Harvard UP, 1998).

29. C.G. Jung and W.E. Pauli, *The Interpretation of Nature and the Psyche* (New York: Ishi Press, 2012).

ic, etc.) as "lines" that are taken up into the complex fabric of the ethical. One could say that one of the things that distinguishes, or at least what ought to distinguish, a complex-integral ethical consciousness is a kind of transparency, within cognition or thinking, to the feeling-tones, somatic processes, and symbolic or imaginal apperceptions that always—though again, usually unconsciously—accompany thinking at all levels of development. I take the metaphor of transparency from Gebser, who uses it to describe a fundamental characteristic of the integral structure, which, in contrast to the deficient mental, has free access to the magical and mythic structures that preceded it, as well as to the mysterious "Origin" (*Ursprung*) that grounds them all.

The efficaciousness of vision-logic or complex thinking as an essential component of a complex-integral ethic depends upon its being embedded within, or expressive of, what Morin describes as a more generalized "psychic culture" wherein the individual, "without being able to cease being egocentric, must elaborate a meta-point of view that allows them to objectify themselves...and to act patiently on themselves: a long apprenticeship and training in reflexivity."[30] Morin draws particular attention to the need for vigilance against the ever-present danger of self-deception and self-justification, which can take such forms as rationalization, selective memory, blinding hatred, or idealizing sentimentality.[31] The cultivation of such a self-reflexive meta-point of view allows us to "evaluate our evaluations, to judge our judgments, and to critique our critiques."[32] To achieve or sustain this meta-point of view demands that the individual come to see and experience themselves as what I have called

30. Morin, *La Méthode: 6,* 102.
31. Ibid., 103.
32. Ibid., 106.

a complex whole.[33] "Every individual," as Morin says, "is unitary, singular, and irreducible. At the same time, however, every individual is double, plural, numberless, and diverse."[34]

> The whole (*ensemble*) constituted by the internal dualities, the plurality of unconscious contents, ... the plurality of separate and mutually ignorant psychic compartments, the well-known but still pertinent division between the head and heart, all of these allow for or determine the paradoxical phenomena of good-bad faith, ... of self-deception, where one succeeds in lying to oneself, in blinding oneself to feelings of embarrassment or hurt.
>
> Lying to oneself reveals our aptitude for splitting (*dédoublement*) and at the same time our aptitude for camouflaging this splitting, since the "I" that lies succeeds in convincing itself of its own sincerity.[35]

While a certain degree of compartmentalization and dissociation is inevitable, and can even, in certain instances (for example, extreme physical or emotional trauma) be understood as a healthy adaptive response, a mature, complex-integral ethical attitude calls for sufficient transparency between the otherwise dissociated terms. It is this transparency that allows for the emergence of the meta-point of view. In the pursuit of such transparency, "the central problem for each individual," writes Morin, "is that of their own internal barbarism."[36]

Where Morin highlights the virtue of reflexivity or "self-critique" as "the best auxiliary in the fight against

33. See S. Kelly, *Individuation and the Absolute: Hegel, Jung, and the Path Toward Wholeness* (New York: Paulist Press, 1993).
34. Morin, *La Méthode: 5*, 73.
35. Ibid., 79.
36. Morin, *La Méthode: 6*, 101.

the illusions of egocentrism,"[37] Wilber stresses the correlative virtue of sincerity or truthfulness for the integrity of the "I." In language reflecting his own creative fusion of depth psychological and hermeneutical traditions, Wilber notes that, according to depth psychology, "at some point in development,"

> ...the person began to deny, repress, distort, conceal, or otherwise "lie" to himself about his own interior status; he began to *mis*-interpret his subjective condition.... A more accurate and faithful *interpretation* of the person's distresses help the person to understand his otherwise baffling symptoms, helps him to see their *meaning*. And thus the person can become less opaque to himself, more transparent and undefended.[38]

The cultivation of a complex-integral ethic has much to learn from psychodynamic perspectives on ego defenses and on strategies for achieving greater integration of the personality. A master concept in this regard is Jung's idea of the shadow. Though the concept of the shadow is most often defined as the inferior part of the personality, Jung sometimes equates it with the more general notion of the personal unconscious, and even the unconscious as a whole. It is the most general term for the inner other, the *alter ego* or "other I"—though in fact, as we saw above, there are many such inner "I's." Wilber has written extensively on the shadow, and has provided a detailed map of developmental stages and their associated pathologies and defenses.[39] Here I would draw attention to his

37. Ibid., 104.
38. K. Wilber, *The Eye of Spirit: An Integral Vision for a World Gone Slightly Mad*, in *The Collected Works of Ken Wilber*, Vol. 7 (Boston: Shambhala, 2000), 431–32.
39. See K. Wilber, "The Developmental Spectrum and Psychopathology: Part I, Stages and Types of Pathology," *The Journal of Transpersonal Psychology* 16.1 (1984): 75–118; K. Wilber, "The Developmental Spectrum and Psychopathology:

helpful encapsulation of the essence of shadow work with his notion of the "3-2-1 process of (re)owning the Self". The process begins with identifying the (usually emotionally charged) dissociated/projected elements (narratively couched in third-person pronouns), entering into conscious dialogue with them (second-person), and finally re-incorporating them as elements of one's own compound individuality or more authentic Self as complex whole. "The therapeutic process," writes Wilber, "consists in turning those 3rd- person monsters (or 'its') back into 2nd-person dialogue voices ('you')... and then going even further and re-identifying with those voices as 1st-person realities that you re-own and re-inhabit using, at that point, 'I' monologues, not voice dialogues."[40] As Wilber notes, the whole process is beautifully suggested, when properly reinterpreted, in Freud's famous phrase: "Where It was, I shall become" (*Wo Es war, Ich soll werden*).

SOCIETY

Though a relatively integrated personality, inwardly transparent to the many and often mutually conflicting part-selves, is necessary for an actualized, third-phase or post-conventional ethical stance, such an integration can only take place in the context of *right relationship with actual others*. Despite his primary emphasis on the need for intra-psychic integration, Jung himself recognized this with his work on the transference (and as we know from his biography, in his intimate life as well).[41] The

Part II, Treatment Modalities," *The Journal of Transpersonal Psychology* 16.1 (1984): 137–66.

40. K. Wilber, *Integral Spirituality: A Startling New Role for Religion in the Modern and Postmodern World* (London: Integral Books, 2007), 136.

41. See L. Owens, *Jung in Love: The* Mysterium *in* Liber Novus (Los Angeles: Gnosis Archive Books, 2015).

idea that healthy ego- or self-development is dependent on healthy relationships with others—to begin with and most consequentially, in the relationship between the infant and the primary care giver—is now widely affirmed and documented by clinicians of early childhood development.[42]

Drawing on Hegel and Habermas, Wilber highlights the degree to which mature self-esteem—a key indicator of a relatively integrated ego—is dependent upon the free flow of inter-subjective relational exchange in the form of mutual recognition. Egoic self-esteem, he writes,

> is actually a *system of mutual exchange*; it is not a self-contained act of invulnerability; even less is it a securing of narcissistic feelings, as maintained by Freudians. For one cannot gain self-esteem without others, and it is actually the *exchange* of esteem with others that *constitutes* true self-esteem. That is, true self-esteem proceeds "on the basis of mutual recognition—namely, on the basis of the knowledge that the identity of the 'I' is possible solely through the identity of the other who recognizes me, and who in turn is dependent on my recognition."[43]

The mutual constitution of inter-subjectivity is crippled as long as one or the other is treated as a mere "it" or object, an insight which Kant enshrined in one of his formulations of the categorical imperative: "Act in such a way that you treat humanity, whether in your own person or in the person of any other, never merely as a means to an end, but always at the same time as an end."

---

42. For a summary of relevant research, see J. Rifkin, *The Empathic Civilization: The Race to Global Consciousness in a World in Crisis* (New York: Tarcher/Penguin, 2009), 47–136.

43. Wilber, *Up from Eden*, 594.

Being treated as an "end" is equivalent to being treated as a subject or person, which usually entails the idea of possessing intrinsic worth or value and of having certain inalienable rights.

To recognize the other as a person, which is to say, as another Self, is to see them with, or through, complex understanding (*compréhension, verstehen*). Insight into the complexity of one's own Self must be extended to the other. "It is an intellectual error," writes Morin, "to reduce a complex whole to only one of its components, but this error is worse in ethics than in science. Here the reduction renders it impossible to understand the other."[44] Thus a new imperative emerges to guide understanding: "Understanding [*compréhension*] rejects rejection, excludes exclusion."[45] More concretely, complex understanding encourages an evolution of the heart-mind away from the self-perpetuating cycle of vengeance, and toward an ethic of magnanimity and forgiveness. There is a boundary, Morin notes, "that separates those, on the one hand, who enclose the criminal within his crime, regardless of what he might have done previously, and especially what he might have become subsequently, and those, on the other hand, who see the possibility of evolution, who believe that criminals can be transformed through repentance, who believe in redemption through this very repentance."[46] When we choose to forget or ignore the ideals of magnanimity, mercy, and forgiveness, he warns, "when we call for punishment as vengeance or as satisfying the talion law, we give way to our internal barbarism."[47]

An ethic of comprehension does not mean that judgment is rendered impossible, only that it must be

---

44. Morin, *La Méthode: 6*, 127.

45. Ibid., 137.

46. Ibid., 144.

47. Ibid., 149.

complexified.[48] Complex understanding

> encompasses explanation, both subjective and objective
> understanding. Complex understanding is multidimen-
> sional: it does not reduce others to a single trait, to a
> single act, and tries to grasp the diverse dimensions or
> aspects of the person in their totality. It tries to insert
> them in their proper contexts and thereby to perceive
> the individual, psychological sources of their behavior
> and thinking, their cultural and social sources, the
> disruptive historical conditions that might have come
> into play.[49]

We could equally say that complex understanding
requires a truly integral approach, which in Wilber's
terms means an AQAL approach—that is, all quadrants
(individual-interior, or Upper Left; individual-exterior,
or Upper Right; collective-interior, or Lower Left; and
collective-exterior, or Lower Right), or some version of
the Big Three ("subjective and objective," "individual,
cultural, and social sources" above), all levels, and all
lines ("traits, dimensions, aspects"). To judge a particular behavior (Upper Right quadrant) adequately, one
needs to know the actor's conscious intention and overall
cognitive-emotional fitness (Upper Left), the worldview
in which the intention is embedded (Lower Left), and
the social (familial, economic, institutional etc.) factors
(Lower Right) that might have conditioned the behavior,
intention, and worldview. Such considerations naturally
enter into the deliberations of lawyers, judges, and juries.
The latter, however, will not be able to enact complex-integral judgments without themselves having attained
adequate levels of cognitive-ethical development.

48. Ibid., 135.
49. Ibid., 126.

UPPER LEFT Individual-Interior First-Person Experience (Awareness) Subjectivity I	**UPPER RIGHT** Individual-Exterior Third-Person Singular Behavior (Physicality) Objectivity IT
WE	ITS
LOWER LEFT Collective-Interior Second-Person Culture (Relationships) Intersubjectivity	**LOWER RIGHT** Collective-Exterior Third-Person Plural Systems (Social Systems and Environment) Interobjectivity

Here we are not so much concerned with judgment of individual behaviors as with the principles and competencies required for a complex-integral ethic proper to the Planetary Era. For Wilber, the inter-objective (Lower Right quadrant) shift from the dominance of nation states to a truly planetary society, in the form of a "pluralistic world-federation," can "only be *seen*, and *understood*, and *implemented*, by individuals with a universal and global vision-logic..."[50] The general trend in cultural transformation, he notes,

> is from the Upper Left of the individual cognitive potential to the Lower-Left of collective worldview, at first marginalized, but finally embedded in Lower-Right social institutions, at which point these basic

50. Wilber, *Sex, Ecology, Spirituality*, 206.

institutions automatically help reproduce the worldview (LL) and socialize the individual (UL) in succeeding generations, acting as "pacers of transformation"—a transformation first started...in a moment of individual creative emergence and transcendence.[51]

The passage above is one of the rare occasions where Wilber describes the dynamics of how the quadrants interact. Instead of the more general recognition that they simply "tetra-interact"—that "they are mutually arising and mutually determining,"[52] what we have is an understanding that they are, in Morin's terms, recursively linked. That is to say, though in this case the initial causal impetus flows from the "cognitive potential" of "individual creative emergence and transcendence," the subsequently transformed worldviews and social institutions in turn shape or feedback upon the cognitive potentials of other individuals, preparing the ground for further creative emergence.

But there are obstacles to the free flow of creative energy between the individual and society. Precisely because each is complexly woven into the other, even if the individual is the locus for the initial causal impetus, it would be futile to target individual transformation without simultaneous attention to worldviews and social praxis. We have already considered the crucial role of early childhood relations with primary caregivers in the formation of a healthy ego, capable of empathic rapport and eventual mutual recognition and complex understanding. Morin, for his part, has emphasized the need for educational reform at all levels. He has outlined the principles of such a reform in his UNESCO sponsored book, *Seven Complex Lessons in Education for the*

51. Ibid., 607.
52. Wilber, *Integral Psychology*, 234.

Future,[53] which summarizes in widely accessible language
the main elements of the paradigm of complexity (including the rudiments of psychic culture, the need to think
in context and with uncertainty, the multidimensional
and complex character of human nature, the history
and challenges of the Planetary Era).[54] It is through such
educational reform that Morin envisions the possibility
of a "cognitive democracy," which he sees as a political-
ly urgent counter to the current situation where deci-
sion-making at all levels of society is left to the experts.
"Hyper-specialization and reduction to the quantifiable,"
Morin laments,

> contribute strongly to the regression of democracy in
> Western countries, where all problems, having become
> technical, elude the grasp of citizens to the profit of the
> experts, and where the loss of global and fundamental
> vision gives free reign not only to the most closed and
> fragmented ideas, but also to the most hollow of global
> ideas and most closed fundamental ideas, including
> and especially those of the technicians and scientists
> themselves.[55]

Unfortunately, with a few notable exceptions, the dominant trend in education continues to be in the direction
of increasing specialization in the service of capitalist
industrial growth society. The latter is informed by a
cultural worldview organized at a deep level by the
deficient mental structure, which, as we have seen, op-
erates according to the dictates of what Wilber calls the

---

53. Morin with Kerne, *Homeland Earth*.

54. About the same time (1996) Wilber published his own popular primer of
integral theory. See K. Wilber, *A Brief History of Everything* (Boston: Shambhala,1996).

55. Morin with Kerne, *Homeland Earth*, 70.

fundamental Enlightenment paradigm, or what Morin terms the paradigm of simplification. This paradigm both informs and is reproduced by what Morin describes as the "four runaway engines" of industrial growth society, each of which is linked in the self-reinforcing loop:

science/technology → economy → profit

a loop which is "propelling spaceship Earth toward the abyss."[56] While each of these terms possesses its own relative autonomy, the first three are in fact largely driven by the last.

The embrace of a genuinely worldcentric or planetary ethic cannot be collapsed into a facile globalism. While global capitalism or Empire is planetary in scope, the world in this case remains a mere theater for the depredations of the ruling elite. As I outlined in the previous chapter, Empire has created, as it is sustained by, a system of planetary apartheid, a planet-wide dominator hierarchy—or system of dominator hierarchies: the 1% over the 99%; "developed" nations over the "developing"; North over South; white over colored; men over women; human over other than human. It is true that capital-driven Empire has brought about the conditions for a certain kind of planetary civilization, to what Morin calls a "global society" (société-monde). However, as Morin notes,

> the [neo]liberal economy... renders impossible the formation of such a society, since it inhibits the constitution of a common legal and governing system and of a common consciousness/conscience.... At a minimum, there must be a reform of the UN, with the goal of a confederation of nations and the democratization of the

56. Morin, La Méthode: 6, 187.

planet. In place of a politics of development, there must be a politics of civilization and a politics of humanity. As both precondition and consequence, there must be a deepening awareness in the human psyche, an awareness both ethical and political, of belonging to the same Homeland Earth.[57]

The shift to a truly planetary ethic, in other words, must involve simultaneous transformation of social structures, individual consciousness, and their underlying worldviews.

NATURE/EARTH

Relative to the idea of the Big Three, the term most frequently linked with individual and society by Morin is "species," by which he means our embeddedness in living organization as it has come to express itself in the organism known as *homo sapiens sapiens*. "Species" in this sense stands for all that we can discern about human nature as a part of nature. Clearly, much depends here on fundamental assumptions about the nature of nature. In the dominant scientific paradigm, nature as a whole, including organisms and arguably human beings as well, is conceived reductively and mechanistically as forms of matter/energy devoid of subjectivity, interiority, and intrinsic value. Though Wilber does not share this view and has proposed a radical critique of what he calls "gross reductionism," something of this view is retained in his characterization of the third term of the Big Three as "It/its." This use of the third (im)person(al) pronoun runs counter to what, as we have seen in previous chapters, Berry and Swimme see as "the central commitment of the Ecozoic"—namely: "That the universe is a communion

57. Ibid., 188–89.

of subjects rather than a collection of objects."[58] Wilber unambiguously shares this commitment, as one can gather from his insistence that all "holons"—all the way down to the most elementary particles—possess interiority and agency, and thus must be approached through both Right- and Left-Hand quadrants. Perhaps some of the confusion could be avoided by replacing the triad of I, We, It/its with that of individual, society, and nature/ Earth, as I am doing here. In any case, with respect to the idea of nature, we can say that the psychotherapeutic axiom, "Where It was, I shall become," must be deepened and extended to include the entire Earth community and, suitably qualified, the cosmos as a whole.

As for the view of nature or the universe as a communion of subjects, one can expect hardy resistance on the part of the mainstream scientific community with respect to elementary particles, atoms, and molecules (I leave aside the common view of all indigenous and most premodern societies, where such things as rivers and mountains, stones, the air, and even human-made objects were often granted a kind of subjectivity or agency). While the dominant trend in the biological sciences continues in the direction of gross reductionism, Morin sees a proto-selfhood (*le Soi*) in all physical systems and processes that manifest a certain closure relative to their environments, beginning with the atom (if not also sub-atomic particles) and including our sun and all stars, galaxies, and everything that whirls and eddies. In

---

58. In this context, we can qualify Morin's claim, quoted earlier, that "It is an intellectual error to reduce a complex whole to only one of its components, but this error is worse in ethics than in science. Here the reduction renders it impossible to understand the other." The qualification in question—and I am confident Morin would assent to it—is that the error is equally bad in science as it is in (human-centered) ethics. Not only does Morin ground human subjectivity in the dynamics of all self-organizing beings, he also rejects the pathological drive to separate science from con-science.

The Nature of Nature and *The Life of Life* (the first two volumes of *Method*), Morin traces the emergence of this physical selfhood out of the complex relation between order, disorder, and organization at both micro and macro levels, and its evolution through dissipative structures to the more complex biological form of selfhood, which he calls *Autos* (from the Greek for "self" or as reflexive pronoun). One of the first to adopt and adapt the idea of self-organization or autopoiesis as formulated by Umberto Maturana and Francesco Varela, Morin provides a detailed and penetrating demonstration of how biological organization, starting with the simplest cell, already manifests a first-person perspective. The action of life is not only productive, but self-productive (metabolism) and reproductive. The organism maintains itself, adapts, propagates, and evolves through enacting choices that have existential import (is this food or poison? a potential mate or an enemy?). The very being of the organism depends upon, and in a real sense is generated by, these choices, which Morin ascribes to what he calls the *computo*—the act of computing in the first person. In a brilliant overturning of Descartes, Morin shows that the more fundamental formula describing the relation of thinking to being would be, not *cogito ergo sum*, but *computo ergo sum*. "The Cartesian *cogito* produces a consciousness of 'am'," writes Morin.

> The *computo*, for its part, produces the *"am,"* which is to say simultaneously the being, existence, and the quality of the subject. The Cartesian *cogito* only knows the I or the Me [that is, the objectified or reflected ego]. There is no Self, that is to say, no corporality, no *physis*, no biological organization in the *cogito*. Moreover, Descartes expels the body into the universe of *res extensa*, itself split off from the immaterial ego; it splits off the living machine and subjectivity from the

"I think". The *computo* necessarily computes together the I, the Me, and the Self, which is to say the physical corporality of the Me-I. The *computo* effects the fundamental unity of the physical, the biological, and the cognitive.... *It reveals to us not only that the idea of the subject cannot be isolated from the living individual, but also that the living individual cannot be isolated from the idea of the subject.* An egocentric, auto-referential, unique, and exclusive affirmation of the subject belongs to every being, to every individual.[59]

The computational agency and individual autonomy of the biological *Autos*—which, as Morin says, is as much cognitive as it is physical and biological—necessarily depends upon what the organism inherits from its ancestors (genetically, and as we now know, epigenetically as well) as well as upon its relations to its environment (food, safe habitat, mate, etc.). We possess genes which possess us, as Morin likes to say. The species (universal or general) reproduces itself through individuals (particular) which reproduce the species. The relation between the individual and the species (between what Morin calls *genos* and *phenon*—the two main poles of *Autos*) are complex, which is to say at once dialogical, recursive, and holographic. It is holographic because of the mutual inclusion of the terms in question (our species includes organisms which include cells which include genes which specify information about the cells which constitute the organisms which constitute the species, etc.). The inclusion is recursive in that the relation between the terms is mutually generative. The individuals embodying a species are particular expressions of the genome as universal. The genome, however, only lives through the ongoing reproduction of individuals. The terms generate

59. E. Morin, *La Méthode 2: La Vie de la Vie* (Paris: Éditions du Seuil, 1980), 190.

each other through a circularly causal or feedback loop. Finally, the relation is dialogical, which means that the terms in question are not only complementary, but also concurrent (that is, relatively autonomous) and potentially antagonistic. Actions that satisfy individual wants or needs can work against the survival of the species, just as actions that favor the species often involve constraints on the behavior of individuals.

The species, of course, and the individuals which constitute it do not exist in a vacuum but are embedded in the many ongoing and complex relations with other species and the abiotic environment. All auto-organizing beings, therefore, are auto-*eco*-organizing beings. Moreover, because the organization is active or ongoing, they are in fact auto-eco-*re*-organizing beings. This leads Morin to the formulation of what he calls the "incompressible paradigm"[60] of *auto-(geno-pheno-ego)-eco-re-organization* required for an adequate understanding of the complex character of living beings. The formula is admittedly unwieldy, especially in this context where I am forced to compress what Morin unfolds over several hundred pages of carefully argued prose.

Morin notes that societies can be conceived as a "third type of individual" (cells being the first type and multicellular organisms the second). In the case of humans, at least, one sees the same complex dynamic between the universal and the particular in biological organization (*genos* and *phenon*) in the socio-cultural (the *genos* pole being evident in all forms of cultural memory). Thus the more complete formulation, a kind of twenty-five syllable mantra that distills the life of life, becomes:

60. Ibid., 351.

auto-(geno-pheno-ego)-socio-(geno-phe-no-ego)-eco-re-organization

Though there are some clear overlaps between Morin's "incompressible paradigm" and Wilber's AQAL map, there are points of incommensurability as well. For instance: "All forms of auto-organization," Morin writes,

> depend not only on their own singular logic or determination, but also on the logic and determinations of their environments. We need to link together in a dialogical—and therefore complex—discourse, explanation from the interior and explanation from the exterior."[61]

Here we seem to have a direct correspondence with Wilber's claim that any integral understanding of living beings, and of all holons, for that matter, must include both Left-(interior) and Right-Hand (exterior) quadrants. In Wilber's classification, however, cells, organisms, societies, and Gaia are all confined to the Right-Hand quadrants (Collective Exterior or "It/its"). This has the effect of occluding the constitutive quality of subjectivity—and thus the constitutive interiority—of all forms of living organization.

A deeper resonance with the ten syllable version of Morin's "incompressible paradigm" (*auto-eco-re-organization*) can be found in Wilber's "twenty tenets" describing the nature of all holons.[62] The first six read as follows:

> 1. Reality as a whole is not composed of things, or processes, but of holons.
> 2. Holons display four fundamental capacities:

---

61. Ibid., 66.
62. See Wilber, *Sex, Ecology, Spirituality*, 43ff.

a. self-preservation
b. self-adaptation
c. self-transcendence
d. self-dissolution

Corresponding to Wilber's "holon" is Morin's "organiza-tion." Tenet 1 a.: self-preservation (in which we could in-clude self-production and reproduction) is a key function of the self- or *auto*-organizing potential of living beings. Self-*adaptation* (tenet 1 b.) clearly corresponds to Morin's *eco*-, while both c. and d. (transcendence/dissolution) correspond to Morin's *re*- (which Morin associates the transformative potential of living organization)[63]. Instead of self-preservation and self-adaptation, Wilber often uses the richer terms *agency* and *communion* (which, inciden-tally, correspond quite nicely with the notions of autopoi-esis and communion in Swimme and Berry's cosmogenetic principle considered in Chapter 3). A holon's agency, he writes,

> its self-asserting, self-preserving, assimilating tenden-cies—express its *wholeness*, its relative autonomy; whereas its communion—its participatory, bonding, joining tendencies—express its *partness*, its relationship to something larger.
>
> Both of these capacities or tendencies are absolutely crucial and equally important; an excess of either will kill a holon immediately (i.e., destroy its identifying pat-tern); even a moderate imbalance will lead to structural deformity (whether we're talking about the growth of a plant or the growth of the patriarchy).[64]

63. See E. Morin, "RE: From Prefix to Paradigm," *World Futures* 61.4 (2005): 254–67.
64. Wilber, *Sex, Ecology, Spirituality*, 49.

The remaining tenets have to do with the nature of holarchical inclusion (emergence and transcendence) and the drive or telos of evolution toward greater depth and complexity. In another writing[65] I have considered the complex character of the relations among ecosphere (physiosphere and biosphere), anthroposphere, and theosphere and highlighted how Morin's insight into the complexity of living organization can help mediate, without dissolving, the tension between Wilber's hierarchical/holarchical and Berry's ecocentric approaches. Bracketing consideration of the theosphere for the moment, we can ask the question as to what extent we might be justified in considering Earth or Gaia as a *fourth* type of individual/subject (after single cells, multi-cellular organisms, and societies). Clearly, in answering this question, much depends on how one defines "Gaia".

As we have seen, Lovelock and Margulis were the first to popularize the idea that Gaia must be understood as a single, self-regulating system whereby life has come to exercise a controlling influence on its abiotic "environment"—most notably, with the chemical composition and dynamic equilibrium of the atmosphere (for the past 200 million years, for instance, with around 21% oxygen and 0.037% CO_2), but also with the salinity and acidity of the oceans and even the composition and behavior of tectonic plates. Though still rejected or resisted by mainstream biologists and geologists, there are compelling reasons to think of Gaia as a single (super)organism, as a living, auto-eco-re-organizing being. If in some non-trivial sense alive, is Gaia therefore, like all other organisms, a subject, not a mere "it" or collection of "its", but an "I" or Self/Autos in her own right? Might not Gaia,

---

65. See S. Kelly, "Five Principles of Integral Ecology," in *The Variety of Integral Ecologies: Nature, Culture, and Knowledge in the Planetary Era*, eds. S. Mickey, S. Kelly, and A. Robbert (Albany: SUNY Press, 2017).

in our own time at least, represent the emergence of a fourth type of individual? As we saw in Chapter 2 with Hans Joachim Schellnhuber, some Earth System scientists, at least, go so far as postulating the existence of a "global subject," albeit one constituted and enacted by the anthroposphere.

Wherever one stands on the metaphysical spectrum with respect to the selfhood of Gaia—with flatland, mechanistic systems thinking on one end (no interiority, no subject), a conscious, personalized world soul (*anima mundi*) on the other, and with Schellnhuber's idea of the global subject somewhere in the middle—one thing is certain: henceforth Earth and humanity must be conceived as a single, indissoluble, complex whole. This is one of the greatest lessons of the Gaianthropocene. It is the lesson of the new field of Earth System science, the mainstream inheritor of Lovelock and Margulis' Gaia Theory. "The new Earth system thinking that emerged fully in the 1990s and 2000s," as Clive Hamilton notes,

> is the integrative meta-science of the whole planet understood as a unified, complex, evolving system beyond the sum of its parts. It is a transdisciplinary and holistic approach assimilating earth sciences and life sciences, as well as the "industrial metabolism" of humankind, all within systems way of thinking, with special focus on the non-linear Dynamics of the system. It represents a markedly novel way of thinking about the Earth that supersedes ecological thinking.[66]
>
> … beyond its scientific importance, the appearance of this new object, the Earth system, has ontological meaning. It invites us to think about the Earth in a new way, an Earth in which it is possible for humankind

---

66. C. Hamilton, *Defiant Earth: The Fate of Humans in the Anthropocene* (Cambridge: Polity, 2017), 12.

to participate directly in its evolution by influencing the constantly changing processes that constitute it. It therefore brings out the conception of a joint human-Earth story...[67]

There will doubtless be multiple contenders for how we should tell this joint human-Earth story. As we saw in Chapter 2, there is currently some tension between the dominant Big History type narratives (which Hamilton describes as "mere causal-chain Big History,"[68] for which any kind of teleology and even the term Gaia are often taboo, and the approach perhaps best represented by Berry, Swimme, and Tucker's "Universe Story." Hamilton, for his part, laments that "we have to confront the most difficult truth—in the Anthropocene we have no ethical resources to draw on."

> Where once we could fear and love God and truly *believe* in him and his saving power, now we can only fear Gaia.... Unless, that is, we can become beings guided by a new cosmological sense rooted in the profound significance of humankind in the arc of the Earth.[69]

Berry, Swimme, and Tucker do not shrink from the idea that life is the telos of matter and mind the telos of life.[70] All three figures (and this goes for integral Gaia theorist, Stephan Harding, as well) not only explicitly embrace more symbolic and expressive modes of communicating the story, but celebrate the idea of an enchanted or numinous cosmos and highlight the deep ethical thrust of the evolutionary process. For them, as for Wilber and Morin,

67. Ibid., 21.
68. Ibid., 116.
69. Ibid., 155–56.
70. See Kelly, "Five Principles of Integral Ecology."

we actually have enormous ethical sources to draw from. "Our human destiny," write Swimme and Tucker,

> is to become the heart of the universe that embraces the whole of the Earth community. We are just a speck in the universe, but we are beings with the capacity to feel comprehensive compassion in the midst of an ocean of intimacy. That is the direction of our becoming more fully human.[71]

"We live in that time," they are bold enough to proclaim, "when Earth itself begins its adventure in self-conscious awareness."[72]

Gaia's self-awakening is coincident with the emergence of a planetary humanity. Correlatively, the planetization of the human throughout the modern or Planetary Era and culminating in our own, post-Anthropocene epoch, is the obverse of the hominization of Earth in the Anthropocene. It is within this unprecedented evolutionary context that we must situate our inquiry into sources of the good.

Ethical Imperatives for the Gaianthropocene

The Gaianthropocene is the occasion for the revelation of a new, this-worldly Trinitarian mystery. The "complex totality" (Morin) that is Gaia is its own kind of "three in One, and One in three." Just as, in traditional mystical Trinitarian speculation and its offshoots (from Augustine through Joachim of Fiore to Hegel, Jung, Pannikar and others), the Godhead is conceived as a paradoxical unity constituted through the complex relations among the three "persons" (in the dominant, patriarchal version: Father,

---

71. Swimme and Tucker, *Journey of the Universe*, 115.
72. Ibid., 109.

Son, and Spirit), so Gaia is best understood in terms of the complex-integral relations among the Big Three of individual, society, and nature/Earth. While each of these three is a relatively autonomous site or source of the good, it is Gaia herself, the entire Earth community, with her own type of hyper- or transjective individuality that constitutes the most comprehensive and concrete source of the good, since it is only here that the complex integrality of the planetary is made explicit. In this sense, in Hegelian terms, we could say that Gaia sublates or both transcends and includes individuals, societies, and nature/Earth. In the new age of the Gaianthropocene, however, the greatest ethical weight falls upon human shoulders, as human actions, for the time being at least, are the most consequential for the entire Earth community. Alongside this practical consideration, it is also the case that it is only in and through the human noosphere—through human cognition and discourse—that we can articulate an ethic adequate to the Gaianthropocene.

It is for this reason that we can agree with Wilber that the noosphere/anthroposphere transcends and, potentially at least, includes the biosphere. I say potentially since, when considering the question of holarchical inclusion, the noosphere/anthroposphere can, and on the whole now largely does, exist in a state of relative dissociation from the biosphere. In many ways, as Hamilton compellingly argues, the human (since 1945 and the Great Acceleration that followed) constitutes an ontological *rupture* relative to the rest of the Earth system.[73] At the same time, the rest of the Earth system retains its autonomy relative to the human, an autonomy that allows it to compensate for the human rupture, to "intrude" (as Isabelle Stengers says) on the illusion of

73. See Hamilton, *Defiant Earth*, 9ff.

human supremacy.[74]

If Earth has evolved to the point where one of its species has become a disruptive force on a planetary scale, a kind of meta-mutation in the evolutionary process itself, humans now have the unique opportunity, and responsibility, to act in the best interests of the Earth community as a whole. In deliberating on the nature of these best interests, the greatest challenge will be to hold true to the complex-integrality of our Gaianthropic Earth community. The key here, says Morin, is to *target concrete universality.* "What stands in the way," he notes, "is due not only to ego- or ethnocentric elements that always sacrifice the general interest to particular interests, but also to a seeming universality, that supposedly knows and serves the general interest, although it is in fact led by an abstract rationality."[75] Such abstract rationality (the "logic of the artificial machine," Gebser's "deficient mental," Wilber's "fundamental Enlightenment paradigm" above) typically takes the form *rationalization*, which, by means of such maneuvers as self-deception (individual) and ideological propaganda (society), masks deeper ego-, ethno-, and sociocentric motivations with false or abstract universals (with the slogan of America as the "Leader of the Free World," to take a glaring, if now thoroughly tattered, example). "The norm of the concrete universal," for its part, "is very difficult to apply."

> The general interest is neither the sum total nor the negation of particular interests. The ecology of action teaches us that action serving the general interest may be diverted in a particular direction. Our notion of

74. See I. Stengers, "The Intrusion of Gaia," in *In Catastrophic Times: Resisting the Coming Barbarism*, translated by Andrew Goffey (Open Humanities Press, 2015), 43–50.
75. Morin with Kerne, *Homeland Earth*, 117.

the general interest should be frequently reexamined with reference to our concrete universe, which is planet Earth.[76]

By "planet Earth," it must be stressed, Morin does not mean nature apart from the human. I have said that we can conceive of Gaia as constituted by the complex (dialogical, recursive, holographic) relations among the Big Three (individual, society, nature). The same can be said for the "levels" of physiosphere, biosphere, and anthroposphere. Echoing his warning about the general interest, "Earth," Morin writes, "is not the sum of an addition: a physical planet, plus the biosphere, plus humankind."

> Earth is a physical/biological/anthropological complex totality, in which life emerges from Earth's history and humankind from earthly life's history. Life is a biophysical organizing force at work in the atmosphere it has created, on the ground, underground, and in the seas, where it has expanded and grown. Humanity [itself] is a planetary and biospheric entity.[77]

Morin's understanding of Earth or Gaia as a complex totality of mutually interpenetrating spheres is in tension with what Wilber sees as hierarchically/holarchically arrayed levels, where, as we see when he says in no uncertain terms, "the biosphere is part of the noosphere, and not vice versa."[78] As I have argued elsewhere, however, short of an a priori commitment to ontological idealism, there is no compelling reason to accept this "not vice versa."[79]

76. Ibid., 117.
77. Ibid., 44.
78. Wilbur, *Sex, Ecology, Spirituality*, 97.
79. See Kelly, "Five Principles of Integral Ecology."

In any case, it is in the context of his AQAL model that Wilber proposes his own overarching ethical imperative, or "Basic Moral Intuition" (BMI), as he calls it. This intuition manifests as "a spiritual Concern for all four quadrants"[80] and takes the following form: *protect and promote the greatest depth for the greatest span.*[81] Depth here refers to levels of interiority (Left-Hand quadrants) and span to levels of exteriority (Right-Hand quadrants). The concern associated the BMI will vary according to the stage of cognitive/affective development from which it is enacted. While the narcissism characteristic of the preconventional moral stage hardly qualifies the intuition as moral, conventional morality extends concern to all members of one's tribe, culture, or nation. With the advent of the postconventional, worldcentric stage, the situation becomes irreversibly complex. Despite the putatively self-evident ("clear and distinct") nature of its ethical universalism—to the Enlightenment mind, at least—it is not long before the critical potential of rationality is enlisted to reveal the abstract and even mendacious character of the universal being invoked. From Wollstonecraft's vindication of the rights of women, through the anti-slavery movement, to post-colonialism, the civil rights movement, and the still growing spectrum of critical theories of race, gender, class, and other forms of oppressively constructed identities, the postconventional might seem to have become completely unmoored from any kind of universal. In fact, however, the emancipatory drive of critique is still guided by the intuition of the universal, since it is precisely such an intuition that highlights the reality of exclusion or oppression (of particulars or singulars not included in the class of the privileged).

80. Ibid., 765.
81. Ibid., 762.

The drive toward the actualization of concrete universality inevitably involves an expansion or extension of concern beyond the human to all sentient beings, to the "land" itself (in Aldo Leopold's sense of the entire biotic community). Whether in struggling with purely human moral dilemmas, such as with the issue of abortion, or with questions relating to the rights or moral standing of animals, rivers, or other features of the non-human world, the ideal or concept of concrete universality may guide, but cannot dictate specific outcomes. The same is true for the basic moral intuition, which is always "unpacked according to the level of the depth of the person doing the intuiting, and is always of the form 'protect and promote the greatest depth for the greatest span' (as best as that person can understand it)."[82] What I have been suggesting, however, if only for pragmatic reasons (though I believe there are compelling theoretical reasons as well) is that Gaia, as concrete universal, is the exemplary embodiment of this intuition.

"The ecological crisis," Wilber claims–"or Gaia's main problem–is not pollution, toxic dumping, ozone depletion, or any such. Gaia's main problem is that not enough human beings have developed to the postconventional, worldcentric, global levels of consciousness, wherein they will automatically be moved to care for the global commons."[83] Making explicit what is already implied by Wilber's Lower Right quadrant developmental sequence (which moves from his more restricted sense of the "Gaian system" as biosphere in the lower levels through tribes and nation states to culminate in the "planetary"), Esbjörn-Hargens and Zimmerman propose the term "planetcentric" instead of worldcentric

82. Ibid., 763.
83. Wilber, Integral Psychology, 137.

to designate the phase shift to a more fully integral, or "post-postconventional" stage of consciousness. As with Morin's understanding of Earth as complex totality and my sense of (integral) Gaia, "the movement of self-identity," they write, "is from egocentric (me) to ethnocentric (me + *my group*) to sociocentric (me + my group + *my nation*) to worldcentric (me + my group + my nation + *all peoples*) to planetcentric (me + my group + my nation + all peoples + *all beings*)."[84]

Though we must remember Morin's warning that Gaia "is not the [mere] sum of an addition: a physical planet, plus the biosphere, plus humankind," Esbjörn-Hargens and Zimmerman's formula does capture the idea of a developmental drive or evolutionary telos toward the actualization of wholeness. While we can speak of the cosmos, God, or the Absolute as *the* Whole, the most encompassing whole of which we have direct acquaintance, and to which we are existentially bound, is Gaia herself. The challenge is how adequately to *think* of, and with and through, this whole. "Never before in the history of humanity," as we will recall, "have the responsibilities of thinking weighed so crushingly on us."[85] The challenge can be met, I believe, through a complex-integral schooling in the ideal of concrete universality, where the concept of holarchical integration is leavened with the ingredients of complexity (especially the dialogic and recursivity). In so doing, the "include" in "transcend and include" associated with the standard (Hegel, Wilber) view of holarchical integration is allowed to work both ways in the whole/part relation (the noosphere includes the biosphere, *and* vice versa).

Alongside the ideal of concrete universality, and in

84. S. Esbjörn-Hargens and M. Zimmerman, *Integral Ecology: Uniting Multiple Perspectives on the Natural World* (London: Integral Books), 617.

85. Morin with Kerne, *Homeland Earth*, 132.

many ways acting, along with the principle of wholeness, as a deeper organizing principle, is the relation between the paired categories of identity and difference. We have already seen how fundamental this relation is to Berry and Swimme's cosmogenetic principle, whose elements "refer to the governing themes and the basal intentionality of all existence."[86] In particular, I drew attention to the manner in which the relation between identity and difference defines the self-organizing character of Gaia or the complex totality of the Earth system in which, as Berry puts it, "we have our most magnificent display of diversity caught up into the coherence of an unparalleled unity."[87] It is in emulation of this "magnificent display" that Morin highlights the following "double imperative, inwardly contradictory but fruitful for that very reason: (a) *everywhere to safeguard, propagate, cultivate, or develop unity;* and (b) *everywhere to safeguard, propagate, cultivate, or develop diversity.*[88] The spirit of this double—and specifically dialogical—imperative finds alternate expression by Morin in the "norm" that he pairs with the injunction to "target concrete universality"—namely, "*To work at what unites, to fight against what separates.*"[89] In this instance, what Morin means by separation is dissociation, disjunction, or pathological differentiation. Because of his wariness of the abstractly totalizing potential of traditional dialectical thinking, Morin avoids any talk of synthesis. Nevertheless, serving the same function as Berry and Swimme's understanding of communion as the third element of the cosmogenetic principle, Morin's affirmation of fellowship, love, and re-liance stand as his versions of a reconciling third term.

86. Swimme and Berry, *The Universe Story*, 71.
87. Berry, *The Sacred Universe*, 115.
88. Morin with Kerne, *Homeland Earth*, 95.
89. Ibid., 117.

Echoing Hegel's early definition of the Absolute as the identity of identity and difference, Morin writes: "Reliance… includes separation. Only the separated can be re-linked. At the level of the human, ethics must operate through fellowship and love, through union in separation, or in other words, the union of union and separation."[90] "The good," he says in no uncertain terms, "is reliance within separation."[91] This good, which applies in equal measure to the individual and to society, is prefigured in the complex auto-eco-re-reorganizational character of life itself. For life, he writes,

> is a teeming of heterogeneities, of excess, dispersion, disorder, antagonism…, error, and blindness, where everything ought "naturally" to decompose, dissociate, disintegrate, disperse; and in fact, everything does naturally decompose and disintegrate in and through death. However, no less "naturally," everything recomposes, re-associates, re-integrates… to form innumerable feed-back loops, cycles, and circuits…. [Thus] the heterogeneous contributes to unity, excess to regulation…, antagonism cooperates with complementarity, …disorder with order… and life begins anew in a teeming of heterogeneities…in the "union of union and disunion."[92]

As concrete universal, the Gaian sphere is both product and productive of these "innumerable feed-back loops, cycles, and circuits." It is only following the emergence of the noosphere, however, with its self-reflexive individuality and symbolically mediated socio-cultural complex-

90. Morin, *La Méthode 6*, 222.

91. Ibid., 114.

92. E. Morin, *La Méthode 3: La Connaissance de la Connaissance* (Paris: Éditions du Seuil, 1986), 371.

ity, that we can speak of the ethical virtues of fellowship, love, and reliance as involving the union of union and separation. "To tap into love," Morin writes, "is to tap into cosmic reliance. Love, the last avatar of reliance, is in fact its most potent and superior form."[93] Love is the "highest expression of the ethical."[94]

Wilber too accords a similar—and in this case, metaphysical as well as cosmological—supremacy to love. Dual in form, love is the true power beneath the integrative potential of vision-logic and the motive force of ethical development, and indeed of holarchical development in general. Drawing from both the Platonic and Christian traditions for his terms, he sees the transcending power of holarchical development as an expression of *Eros*, and its power of inclusion as an expression of *Agape*. Together, they constitute a "Great Circle" of ascent (Eros) and descent (Agape). Wilber summarizes the movement of this Great Circle with the phrase: "flee the Many, find the One; having found the One, embrace the Many *as* the One."[95] Or in shorter form: "Return to One, embrace the Many."[96]

One does not have to subscribe to the Neo-Platonist metaphysics of eternal, supraphysical forms to affirm the more general idea of love as evolutionary driver or ethical ultimate. Though Morin eschews metaphysical pronouncements, preferring instead to ground his "Great Circle" in the complex (dialogical, holographic, and recursive) cycles of life, his dual imperative—(a) *everywhere to safeguard, propagate, cultivate, or develop unity;* and (b) *everywhere to safeguard, propagate, cultivate, or develop diversity*—echoes Wilber's integral take on the

93. Morin, *La Méthode 6*, 35.
94. Ibid., 34.
95. Wilber, *Sex, Ecology, Spirituality*, 326.
96. Ibid.

classic metaphysical problem of the One and the Many. Despite his avoidance of metaphysics, moreover, Morin does recognize, and even celebrate, the fact that, "[b]ecause it harbors within itself the principle of incompleteness, complex thinking allows for a mysterious reinforcement of the Mystery."[97] This Mystery is evidently related to the fourth source of the Good alluded to at the beginning of this chapter when Morin asks: "Might there not also be, beneath this anthropological layer [following that of the individual and of society], a quasi-primordial re-sourcing and re-liance that puts us in touch with the fifteen-billion-year distant origin of the universe itself?"[98] Whatever this origin and Mystery might be in themselves, Morin leaves to the metaphysicians. This side of the Mystery, however, he is more than willing to recommend, as perhaps his most concentrated ethical imperative—"*aimez pour vivre, vivez pour aimer!*"[99] which might be translated as: *love for the sake of life, live for the sake of love!* He adds: "Love the fragile and perishable, for the best and most precious of things—including consciousness, beauty, and the soul—are fragile and perishable."[100] Morin's existential emphasis on the transitory and finite, his passionate commitment to the plane of immanence, is in tension with the vein of transcendence that runs through the great Axial traditions, whether religious or philosophical. The same could be said with respect to Wilber's affirmation of Spirit. In fact, however, Wilber's version of integral nondualism can arguably accommodate this emphasis, at least on pragmatic grounds. "Can we not ... see," he asks, "that Spirit always manifests in all four quadrants equally? Is

---

97. Morin, *La Méthode 5*, 272.
98. Morin, *La Méthode 6*, 26.
99. Ibid., 232.
100 Ibid.

not Spirit here and now in all its radiant glory, eternally present in every I and every We and every It? Will not our more adequate interpretations of Spirit facilitate Spirit's rescue of us?"[101]

Though I will not hold out for any kind of rescue, I am committed to more adequate interpretations of Spirit, ones that arise out of, and might better assist us in navigating, these critical years of the dawning Gaianthropocene.

101. Wilber, *Sex, Ecology, Spirituality*, 549.

5

The Paradox of Planetary Initiation

But the life of Spirit is not the life that shrinks from death and keeps itself untouched by devastation, but rather the life that endures it and maintains itself in it. It wins its truth only when, in utter dismemberment, it finds itself.
—Hegel

The death/birth struggle is perhaps the way, through infinite risks, toward the general metamorphosis—on the condition that we raise to consciousness this very struggle.
—Edgar Morin

I RETURN IN THIS CHAPTER to the observation which opened the first: that the entire Earth community is poised on the threshold of what amounts to a planetary rite of passage, an initiatory journey with its own collective Near Death Experience (NDE). While implicit in some of C.G. Jung's later pronouncements, Richard Tarnas (drawing from Jung, Joseph Campbell, and Stanislav Grof) is one of the first to have made the explicit connection between our planetary predicament and the process of initiation. In a lecture in 1997, then in a 2001 essay, "Is the Modern Psyche Undergoing a Rite of Passage?", Tarnas noted:

> I believe that humankind has entered into the most critical stages of a death-rebirth mystery. In retrospect it seems that the entire path of Western civilization has taken humankind and the planet on a trajectory of initiatory transformation, into a state of spiritual alienation, into an encounter with mortality on a global scale—from world wars and holocausts to the

nuclear crisis and now the planetary ecological crisis—
an encounter with mortality that is no longer individual and personal but rather transpersonal, collective,
planetary.[1]

Though compelling at the time to those in our community, this pronouncement was still mostly a voice crying
in the wilderness. More than twenty years later, however,
prophecy has become the stuff of daily news. Along with
the tens of millions of refugees or those trapped in war
zones, poverty, or facing other forms of existential threat,
great swathes of the general public now sense something
of the nearness of death in the accelerating planetary
emergency, with climate chaos and the mass extinction of
species as its most telling manifestations.[2]

One of the things I want to draw out here is the
paradoxical quality—we could also say the complex
character—of this looming collective NDE. It is genuinely
paradoxical, I believe, because there seems to be no rational solution to the contradictions involved. These contradictions and complexities are not merely theoretical in
nature. They are also being embodied and acted out in
the tensions between different activist communities. Since
these communities nevertheless share fundamental values
and even many of the same goals, I offer these reflections
with the hope that these communities might maximize
their synergistic potential as allies in confronting the truly apocalyptic character of our planetary moment.

Before returning to the idea of planetary initiation, I want to note the growing tension between those

1. R. Tarnas, "Is the Modern Psyche Undergoing a Rite of Passage?", *Cosmos and Psyche*, 2001, 18, https://cosmosandpsyche.files.wordpress.com/2013/05/revision-rite-of-passage.pdf (accessed May 3, 2020).

2. Though uncertain in its ultimate consequences, at the time of writing, the COVID-19 global pandemic has added another, more immediate, layer to this sense of existential threat.

who believe that civilizational collapse and ecological catastrophe are inevitable (and even already well underway) and those who insist on the real possibility of transitioning to some form of ecological civilization. Both groups agree on key facts: the existential threat of climate chaos, the accelerating mass extinction of species, and the various disruptions to human existence already in evidence (failed states, forced migrations, growing economic disparities, the rise of malignant nationalisms and totalitarianism, global pandemics, etc.). On the question of climate change, there is some disagreement on projected upper limits and timing of possible warming. The current IPCC consensus warns of the risk of business as usual leading to between 3 and 5 degrees C by 2100, but includes the assertion that there is still time to avoid catastrophe. Others, by contrast, cite the history of IPCC projections being consistently conservative, over-optimistic, and of ignoring crucial feedback mechanisms (notably, arctic methane), and warn of the possibility of between 3 and 8 or more degrees C from as early as 2050. Those who rely on the official consensus view of the IPCC also highlight the many strategies for possible drawdown of atmospheric carbon (and actually depend upon the successful implementation of these strategies for their projections). Though supportive of many of these strategies, the more pessimistic (realistic?) assessments tend to regard them as too little, too late.

Here I am not interested in arguing the case for or against the official consensus that, despite the IPCC having raised the threat alert considerably in its most recent reports, it is still possible to avoid the apocalyptic phase shift into "Hothouse Earth." Instead, I am more concerned with exploring deeper psychospiritual factors that might be catalyzing, and catalyzed by, the views of both camps. Since members of both camps make use of the same data sets, the fact that they come to significantly different conclusions suggests that non-empirical and even non-rational factors are at play, factors which reside at the level of individual temperament, psychological type, or worldview. In the following reflections on these factors, I follow Tarnas's lead in drawing from the insights of transpersonal psychology, in particular from the work of William James, C.G. Jung, and especially Stanislav Grof.

Temperamental Differences

Addressing the question of temperament, William James proposed a divide between what he called the "tough" and the "tender" minded, where the former are typically guided in their views by appealing to empirical facts or concrete reality (often of a limiting character), while the latter appeal to ideals and principles (often stressing possibility). Ignoring the details of James's characterization, Jung pointed out resonances between these two types and his own fundamental typological distinction between extraverts and introverts.[3] In the case at hand, we might consider those still clinging to some kind of hope in face of the worsening planetary emergency to be more tender-minded or introverted. This kind of typological distinction is only partially revealing, however, as the hopeful also appeal to their own sets of facts. At the same time, not all introverts are optimistic, just as not all extraverts are pessimistic. Something more, something deeper is at play here.

In his phenomenological investigation of the varieties of religious experience, James proposed a somewhat analogous, though more complex, typological distinction relative to the question of evil, the nature of the divine, and the fundamental constitution of the cosmos, this time between two mutually incompatible worldviews:

3. See Jung, *Psychological Types* (Princeton UP, 1976), 502f..

the "healthy-minded" and the "sick-souled." I cannot
do justice to James's treatment of these worldviews,
which, along with its conceptual and expressive richness,
is grounded in a wide selection of representative religious, philosophical, and literary sources. In general, if
the sick-souled person is vulnerable to melancholy and
pessimism, the healthy-minded possesses a "temperament
organically weighted on the side of cheer and fatally for-
bidden to linger, as those of opposite temperament linger,
over the darker aspects of the universe."[4] Though less
prone to depression, pessimism, and fatalism, in some
healthy-minded individuals "optimism may become qua-
si-pathological. The capacity for even a transient sadness
or a momentary humility seems cut off from them as by
a kind of congenital anesthesia..."[5] Once again, though I
have met individuals for whom this typological distinction seems to hold, with respect to the two communities
of climate (and more generally social and ecological)
activists I am in touch with, the reality is more complex.
For instance, I know people who, though passionate
advocates for "active" or "radical" hope, by no means
gloss over the horror of our planetary predicament. By
the same token, those who have abandoned all hope
for the transition to an ecological civilization are not all
depressed, fatalistic, or mired in the darker realities of
our collective moment. Still, there is something to James's
proposal. Perhaps, as James himself recognizes, since
human personality is not monolithic, but rather multiple and complex by nature, we can think of these two
worldviews as poles or attractors that exert their power
differentially, from individual to individual, and from
context to context. As worldviews, however, there is no

4. W. James, *The Varieties of Religious Experience* (New York: Penguin, 1982), 83.
5. Ibid.

doubt as to which James considers superior. "It seems to me that we are bound to say," he concludes,

> that morbid-mindedness ranges over the wider scale of experience, and that its survey is the one that overlaps. The method of averting one's attention from evil, and living simply in the light of good is splendid as long as it will work. It will work with many persons; it will work far more generally than most of us are ready to suppose; and within the sphere of its successful operation there is nothing to be said against it as a religious solution. But it breaks down impotently as soon as melancholy comes; and even though one be quite free from melancholy one's self, there is no doubt that healthy-mindedness is inadequate as a philosophical doctrine, because the evil facts which it refuses positively to account for are a genuine portion of reality; and they may after all be the best key to life's significance, and possibly the only openers of our eyes to the deepest levels of truth...[6]

And where might we turn for insight into these "deepest levels of truth?" Here I would suggest that we follow the evolution of transpersonal psychology from James to the depth-psychological perspectives of Jung and Grof. James himself indicates a direction to follow with his appeal in the *Varieties* to the metaphor of the "twice-born." Though sometimes seeming to equate the twice-born with the sick-souled, we can in fact imagine both healthy-minded and sick-souled individuals having experienced the kind of psychospiritual transformation signaled by the metaphor of a second birth (if even James himself focuses on the transformation of the sick-soul).

6. Ibid., 163.

The Death-Rebirth Archetype

The metaphor of birth and its symbolic equivalents are ubiquitous in human cultural expression and have played a prominent role in the realms of myth and ritual. This is especially true in the case of rituals of initiation or rites of passage, where it is always the case of an individual transitioning from one identity—or more precisely dying to that identity—and being refashioned or born into a new identity. As I noted in Chapter 1, rites of passage are common at key points of transition in the life cycle: birth, puberty, marriage, elderhood, death, but also whenever there is a transition to a new socially sanctioned role or identity (chief, king or queen, shaman, healer, etc.). The universality and numinosity (that is, the powerful energetic charge at the level of experience) of rites of passage is a clear indication of their archetypal character. One could say that the archetype in question is that of Life itself in its specifically human form, which Jung also refers to as the archetype of the Self. By Self we can understand the wholeness of personality or the psyche as a vehicle for the creation of consciousness. Like everything that lives—from single cells to complex organisms and arguably Gaia or the planet as a whole—the Self is a dynamically self-organizing totality. The various phases in the life cycle of the Self constitute so many births, deaths, and rebirths.[7]

Clearly, as biological beings, the prototypical occasion we all have for experiencing the deep structure of the Self is in the actual process of being born. One of Stanislav Grof's major contributions to depth psychology was his

---

7. Though Jung understandably identifies life with the archetype of the *anima*, I believe that, insofar as both can be defined in terms of self-organization (autopoiesis) and what I have called the principle of complex holism (see Kelly, *Individuation and the Absolute*), life corresponds more precisely with the archetype of the Self. Echoing Hegel's early definition of the Absolute as the "identity of identity and non-identity" as well as Jung's definition of the Self as a *complexio oppositorum*, Morin remarks that "All the great developments of life came about

elucidation of the nature and significance of the perinatal process (that is, the entire process surrounding birth, from gestation to delivery).[8] Because biological birth marks the experiential initiation of the individual into the world of the separate-self sense and involves a simultaneous death to the participatory consciousness of intra-uterine existence, the perinatal experience becomes the prototype of all subsequent major life transformations. "Perinatal experiences," writes Grof,

by means of the recuperation and, in a sense, the integration of death." Life, he continues, "is a teeming of heterogeneities, of excess, dispersion, disorder, antagonism..., error, and blindness, where everything ought 'naturally' to decompose, dissociate, disintegrate, disperse; and in fact, everything does naturally decompose and disintegrate in and through death. However, no less 'naturally', everything recomposes, re-associates, re-integrates... to form innumerable feedback loops, cycles, and circuits.... [Thus] the heterogeneous contributes to unity, excess to regulation..., antagonism cooperates with complementarity, ...disorder with order... and life begins anew in a teeming of heterogeneities...in the 'union of union and disunion'." Morin, *La Méthode 2: La Vie de la Vie* (Paris: Éditions du Seuil, 1980), 371 and 397.

8. Grof is rightly considered by many in the transpersonal field as the most significant figure in the depth-psychological tradition following Jung. Trained as a psychiatrist and classical psychoanalyst, Grof pioneered the clinical use of LSD in the '50s and '60s in Czechoslovakia and the United States. His original motive for using LSD and other psychedelic drugs was "to explore their potential to intensify, deepen, and accelerate the therapeutic process in Freudian analysis." S. Grof, "Modern Consciousness Research and Human Survival," in *Human Survival and Consciousness Evolution*, eds. S. Grof with M.L. Valier (Albany: SUNY, 1988), 58. The experiences which surfaced, however, soon convinced him of the inadequacy of Freud's model of the psyche. Not only were the subjects consistently reporting experiences which clearly transcended the biographical domain of childhood traumas, but it was these, trans-biographical experiences which seemed to have the highest therapeutic value (which, incidentally, confirms Jung's insight into the essential links between healing, wholeness, and the holy). Following the legal ban on the clinical use of psychedelics, Stan and Christina Grof developed a nonpharmacological approach—combining deep, accelerated breathing with evocative music and focused body work—an approach they call "holotropic therapy," which has confirmed and extended the previous research. See Grof, *The Adventure of Self-Discovery: Dimensions of Consciousness and New Perspectives in Psychotherapy and Inner Exploration* (Albany: SUNY, 1988) as well as *The Way of the Psychonaut: Encyclopedia for Inner Journeys.* (Multidisciplinary Association for Psychedelic Studies, 2020).

seem to represent an intersection or frontier between the personal and the transpersonal—a fact reflected in their connection with birth and death, the beginning and end of individual existence. Transpersonal phenomena reveal connections between the individual and the cosmos that seem at present beyond comprehension. All we can say in this respect is that, somewhere in the process of perinatal unfolding, a strange qualitative Moebiuslike leap seems to occur in which deep exploration of the individual unconscious turns into a process of experiential adventure in the universe-at-large, involving what can best be described as the superconscious mind.[9]

Familiarity with the phenomenology of the perinatal process can provide invaluable insights into the nature of all processes of deep transformation, whether individual or collective. The perinatal process comprises three main phases: from the long period of (ideally) relatively undisturbed gestation, through the shorter period of labor, to the shortest period of actual delivery. These three phases correspond to the more general developmental logic (as typified in the Hegelian dialectic) of movement from a state of initial identity, through a phase of differentiation, to the emergence of a new identity.[10] We see the same logic at work in Jung's theory of individuation with the movement from an initial identification with the collective unconscious, through the differentiation of the personal ego, to the emergence of the Self as the more actualized expression of the wholeness of personality.[11]

9. S. Grof, *Beyond the Brain: Birth, Death and Transcendence in Psychotherapy* (Albany: SUNY, 1985), 127.

10. See Kelly, *Coming Home*, 18f., 119f.

11. Though unaware of each other's work at the time, Tarnas (1992) and I (1993) had each drawn attention to the shared deep structure of Hegel's dialectical logic

The Perinatal Process

Overlaying this triphasic developmental logic, Grof identified four distinct phenomenological gestalts or patterns in the perinatal process, calling them *Basic Perinatal Matrices* (BPM). While Grof's understanding of the perinatal is strongly informed by the actual phenomenology of biological birth, it is essential from the start to recognize the *meta*-natal character of the perinatal, for it is primarily to the archetypal or "deep" structure of birth that perinatal theory is addressed. "In spite of its close connection to childbirth," as Grof says, "the perinatal process transcends biology and has important psychological, philosophical, and spiritual dimensions."[12] It is with the deep structure of these dimensions in mind that Grof proposed his model of the four Basic Perinatal Matrices. The word "matrix" here is particularly apposite since, along with its literal meaning of "mother" and "womb," it suggests as well the function of a mold (as in printing or in engineering) or a set (as in mathematics), both of which connote the "meta" qualities of potentiality and universality.

In the context of biological birth, BPM I corresponds to the period from conception to just before the onset of labor and is governed by the principle of identity or original participation with the maternal organism. With BPM II, though labor has begun, the cervix is still closed, thus key experiential correlates to this matrix include the feeling of "no exit" from overwhelming distress, depression, hopelessness, and meaninglessness. In BPM III the cervix is open and the fetus can participate actively in the birth process. This phase, however, also typically includes

of the evolution of consciousness and Jung's understanding of individuation. Tarnas was the first to point out how this same deep structure undergirds Grof's model of the perinatal process and to apply the latter, so interpreted, to the evolution of the western mind.

12. Grof, *The Adventure of Self-Discovery*, 9.

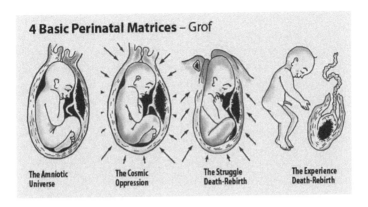

4 Basic Perinatal Matrices – Grof

The Amniotic Universe | The Cosmic Oppression | The Struggle Death-Rebirth | The Experience Death-Rebirth

crushing pressures, hyperstimulation, and the real possibility of death through suffocation, and thus Grof often refers to this matrix as the "death-rebirth struggle." BPM IV corresponds to actual delivery, which, if all goes well, involves the "death-rebirth experience," where the individual dies to the prior state of identity with the mother and is born as a biologically autonomous (if still initially utterly dependent) being. Here we have the core paradox of the perinatal process—being born involves what amounts to a near-death experience.

Recognition of the archetypal character of the perinatal process helps us understand the powerful, irrational (or a-rational) charge that often accompanies whatever processes or situations that participate in its deep structure. We can attribute a significant portion of this charge to residual and unprocessed trauma from our own individual births. As early as 1975 in *Realms of the Human Unconscious* and in subsequent publications, Grof provided penetrating insights into the possible role of residual trauma in the prevalence of violence, greed, and related pathological behavior in times of war and more generally in the context of the accelerating planetary crisis. "Individuals involved in systematic self-exploration," he observed in 1985, frequently develop, quite independently from each other, convincing insights that humanity at large is facing these days a serious dilemma fully comparable to that described for the process of individual transformation. The alternatives involved seem to be continuation of the present trend toward exteriorization, acting out, and external manipulation of the world, or turning within and undergoing process of radical transformation to an entirely new level of consciousness and awareness. While the easily predictable end result of the former strategy is death in an atomic war or in technological waste products, the latter alternative could result in evolutionary perspectives described in the writings of Sri Aurobindo, Teilhard de Chardin, Ken Wilber, and many others.[13]

Because the perinatal process is archetypal, its energetic charge should also be understood as emanating from a collective field at the species level. This field, though to a certain extent generated or at least energized by the cumulative residue of the birth experience of countless individuals, itself resonates with the fields of all living or developmental phenomena. Stars and trees and whales, seasons, days, and intimate relationships all participate in the same archetype of Life and its tri- or quadriphasic deep structure. We can therefore expect a strong resonance not only in the case of individuals explicitly engaged in rites of passage (a rarity in our times) or their experiential analogues, but with our current planetary predicament as a whole insofar as it approximates a collective initiation. More precisely, we can expect a complex reinforcing feedback between and among individuals, the social collective, and the emergent planetary identity in the making, all catalyzed by, as they in turn

13. Grof, *Beyond the Brain*, 429.

catalyze, the underlying archetypal dynamics of the perinatal process.

Here, as in so many other respects, my thinking is very close to that of Tarnas, who makes essentially the same point in the epilogue to *The Passion of the Western Mind*.[14] It also overlaps in significant respects with that of Christopher Bache, who has proposed some friendly modifications to Grof's perinatal model. While Grof drew out crucial implications of residual birth trauma to the planetary crisis, his focus remained largely on individual consciousness. Following Grof's own understanding of the archetypal character and transpersonal dimensions of the perinatal process, Bache focuses on and develops what is already assumed by Grof (and Jung, for that matter, with his theory of the collective unconscious) and acknowledged by Tarnas—namely, the idea of a *species mind* in which the individual mind or psyche participates. More particularly, Bache suggests that part of the reason, at least, why experiential engagement of the perinatal unconscious is generally so overwhelming is that, in revisiting one's own unprocessed birth trauma, the psyche resonates with a corresponding perinatal dimension of the species mind. This dimension of the greater Mind (again, one can think here of the Jungian idea of the collective unconscious) functions as the repository not only of humanity's cumulative experience of biological birth, but also (as Grof demonstrates for the case of

14. Tarnas notes, for example, that "[t]his archetypal dialectic was often experienced simultaneously on both an individual level and, often more powerfully, a collective level, so that the movement from primordial unity through alienation to liberating resolution was experienced in terms of the evolution of an entire culture, for example, or of humankind as a whole—the birth of Homo sapiens ... Here personal and transpersonal were equally present, inextricably fused, so that ontogeny not only recapitulated phylogeny but in some sense opened out into it.... this archetypal dialectic was experienced or registered in several dimensions—physical, psychological, intellectual, spiritual—often more than one of these at a time, and sometimes all simultaneously " (*Passion*, 429).

the individual) of all unprocessed traumatic residues that
share the same feeling tone or other phenomenological
qualities as one or more of the various phases or matrices
(or "Meta-Matrices," as Bache calls them) of the birth
process. Participating in the same informational field,
these experiences and residues are all non-locally related
and potentially accessible (especially in non-ordinary
states of consciousness) by what Rupert Sheldrake has
called "morphic resonance."[15] Given these assumptions,
Bache proposes the following:

> ...just as problematic experiences can collect and
> block the healthy functioning of the individual, similar
> blockages might also occur at the collective level. This
> suggests that the unresolved anguish of human history
> might still be active in the memory of the species-mind,
> burdening its life just as our individual unresolved
> anguish burdens ours. Continuing the parallel, if con-
> scious engagement of previously unresolved pain brings
> therapeutic release at the personal level, the same might
> also occur at the species level.[16]

It is difficult to see at this point in time how Bache's
claims regarding therapeutic release at the species level could be verified, which does not, however, mean
they should not be pursued (especially given the stakes
involved). What I would stress here, however, and as
Tarnas emphasizes in the epilogue to *Passion*, is that the
perinatal dimension of the species mind not only functions as repository of cumulative trauma, but points as
well to the notion that our species is itself undergoing a
kind of birth and evolutionary leap. This implies that,

15. R. Sheldrake, The *Presence of the Past: Morphic Resonance and the Habits of Nature* (New York: Times Books, 1988).

16. C. Bache, *Dark Night, Early Dawn* (Albany: SUNY Press, 2000), 78.

along with the idea that it might be necessary for enough of us to do the work of inner transformation to make a difference at the level of socio-political reality (as Grof maintains), such a difference would conceivably involve both a catharsis and an awakening of the species mind itself. More particularly, as I am arguing in this and other chapters, along with considering the interactions between individual consciousness and the species mind, it is a question of the supraordinate mind or psyche of the planet as a whole, the *anima mundi* or Gaian Self that is engaged in its own initiatory perinatal process.[17]

Notes from the Field

As tensions continue to mount with each new report of rising temperature and levels of CO_2, of melting ice, raging fires, plummeting wildlife populations, global pandemics, and signs of civilizational collapse, it should not surprise us to find intensified expressions of BPM II and III, on the one hand, and a longing for the deliverance of BPM IV (or the fantasy of return to BPM I), on the other. Because the entire Earth community is caught up in the archetypal process of initiation, as Tarnas had already noted some twenty years ago, we find ourselves sealed inside "a psychic pressure cooker, an alchemical vessel that is intensifying the archetypal energies into a collective morphic field of explosive power."[18]

How might these energies be manifesting in the general public and with respect to the tension among activist communities I began with? One does not have to go far to look for expressions of key characteristics of the experiential gestalt associated with BPM II. In the United

17. Or more precisely, rather than the *anima mundi*, we could say that it is the planetary ego (or *Weltgeist*) that is undergoing the initiation (for my proposed distinction between the two terms, see *Coming Home*, 171f.).

18. Tarnas, "Is the Modern Psyche Undergoing a Rite of Passage?", 18

States alone, for instance, a 2016 study revealed a stunning rise of 33% in diagnosed cases of major depression since 2013, with the highest rates occurring among teens and young adults. Girls and women were twice as likely as boys and men to suffer from major depression.[19] While many factors can be adduced in accounting for this rise, alongside and amplifying such specific factors as deteriorating social relations in connection with addiction to social media and digital culture, one can reasonably assume that youth, girls, and women—as the carriers of future life—are especially sensitive (if even unconsciously) to the mounting signs of planetary catastrophe. As of 2017, suicide rates were highest in the United States since World War II, with the highest rates among American Indians and Alaska natives. Boys and girls age 10 to 14 have seen the largest rate increase.[20] Suicide is a desperate last resort response to the crippling feeling of hopelessness and "no exit" typical of BPM II.

A more general indicator of the activation of BPM II is the rise in the collective consciousness of the threat of both civilizational collapse and human extinction, and more particularly in those cases that consider them to be both inevitable and relatively immanent. The Doomsday Clock of the Bulletin of the Atomic Scientists, which now pairs climate change with the threat of nuclear annihilation, was advanced in 2020 to one hundred seconds before

19. M. Fox, "Major Depression on the Rise Among Everyone, New Data Shows," NBC News, May 10, 2018, https://www.nbcnews.com/health/health-news/major-depression-rise-among-everyone-new-data-shows-n873146 (accessed May 3, 2020). See also Blue Cross Blue Shield, "Major Depression: The Impact on Overall Health," May 10, 2018, https://www.bcbs.com/sites/default/files/file-attachments/health-of-america-report/HoA_Major_Depression_Report.pdf (accessed May 3, 2020).

20. J. Ducharme, "US Suicide Rates Are the Highest They've Been Since World War II," Time, June 20, 2019, https://time.com/5609124/us-suicide-rate-increase/ (accessed May 3, 2020).

midnight. At about the same time, the UN and the IPCC announced that there were only "12 years" left "to limit climate change catastrophe," with apocalyptic warnings of "extreme heat, drought, floods and poverty."[21] Since then we have witnessed a rising tide of reports (too many to list here) lamenting previous underestimations of the threats we face, moving forward former deadlines, and documenting the arrival of the dreaded Four Horsemen.

Our intensifying planetary predicament is more complex than an individual birth in that all four Basic Perinatal Matrices are simultaneously at play. Experiential and behavioral features associated both with BPM IV (delivery) and BPM I (effortless fusion with the nurturing womb), are clearly in evidence in the case of responses to the accelerating planetary crisis which seek to avoid feelings of distress through fantasies of escape, whether to a terraformed Mars, the dream of limitless, "free" energy, or other technotopian or transhumanist visions of a reconfigured Earth where all natural constraints are overcome and all of our physical needs are met (the so-called technological Singularity). At the extreme of this kind of response one finds such beliefs as the confident expectation of intervention on part of benevolent alien civilizations (who, on the analogy of an emergency C-section delivery, are thought to be the holders of the advanced technology that will save us from the brink). Then there are the contemporary inheritors of the New Thought movement that provided the model for James's portrait of the Healthy-Minded type of individual, such as the proponents of the so-called "Law of Attraction," who consider it taboo to dwell on "negative" visions of our future (or the present), insist-

21. J. Watts, "We Have 12 Years to Limit Climate Change Catastrophe, Warns UN," *The Guardian*, October 8, 2018, https://www.theguardian.com/environment/2018/oct/08/global-warming-must-not-exceed-15c-warns-landmark-un-report (accessed May 3, 2020).

ing that focusing only on images of universal abundance will magically bring us to the promised land.[22] I will have something to say about positive features of BPM I along with less delusional appeals to the power of positive thinking in the concluding section.

Returning to the dynamics of BPM II, Tarnas noted in an interview that

> The part of the perinatal experience where the cervix is closed, but the contractions are happening and it seems like there is no way out: there can be such a catastrophic sense that one is never going to get out, that one is the victim of endless meaningless suffering. But if one stays with this intolerable state, this crucifixion—much as Jung talked about it, you have to surrender yourself to the crucifixion between the opposites—then something can unfold that will re-contextualize it in a way that opens up to a whole new dimension of being and understanding.[23]

We seem to be witnessing just such a recontextualization insofar as, alongside and perhaps in response to

22. See for instance this post from a believer in the Law of Attraction: "Keep affirming. The planet is in harmony. Earth is in harmony. Nature is protected. The solutions are found. And I keep seeing more and more positive headlines of people finding crazy new solutions, like how to regrow coral, plastic-eating fungus, countries banning deforestation, a couple replanting an entire forest, etc. Keep imagining and visualizing Heaven and Utopia on Earth. Rest easy in this space as you sleep. It's here." Buffybison, "Can We Heal this Planet/Stop Climate Change with Law of Attraction?", *Reddit*, June 12, 2019, https://www. reddit.com/r/lawofattraction/comments/bzaejf/can_we_heal_this_planet-stop_climate_change_with/ (accessed May 3, 2020). For an especially egregious example of this kind of delusion, see: R. Cragwall, "All Beliefs Are Self Imposed – Even Climate Change," *The Law of the Promised*, June 9, 2017, https://thelaw-thepromisecom.wordpress.com/2017/06/09/all-beliefs-are-self-imposed-even-climate-change/ (accessed May 3, 2020).

23. K. Olivetti, "Dimensions of the Psyche: A Conversation with Stanislav Grof, M.D., and Richard Tarnas, Ph.D.," *The Jung Journal: Culture and Psyche* 9.4 (2015): 98–124

the despair and hopelessness of BPM II, there has been a remarkable upsurge of activism surpassing the great protests and mobilizations of the 60's. The fall of 2019 saw the unprecedented rise of the global youth climate protest movement catalyzed by the iconic Greta Thunberg. "Rarely, if ever," the *New York Times* reported, "has the modern world witnessed a youth movement so large and wide, spanning across societies rich and poor, tied together by a common if inchoate sense of rage."[24] Pointedly encapsulating the instinctive impulse to act in face of existential threat—an impulse typically associated with *the death-rebirth struggle* of BPM III—Greta addressed the World Economic Forum in Davos as follows:

> Adults keep saying: "We owe it to the young people to give them hope." But I don't want your hope. I don't want you to be hopeful. I want you to panic. I want you to feel the fear I feel every day. And then I want you to act.
>
> I want you to act as you would in a crisis. I want you to act as if our house is on fire. Because it is.[25]

In the case of traditional initiations, the individual can at least take some consolation in knowing that others have succeeded in coming through the other side of the death-rebirth struggle, including that of our own births. The initiand can in this sense legitimately cling to some kind of hope. Greta's admonition, however, is actually more in tune with what the fetus must experience strug-

24. S. Sengupta, "Protesting Climate Change, Young People Take to Streets in a Global Strike," *New York Times*, September 20, 2019, https://www.nytimes.com/2019/09/20/climate/global-climate-strike.html (accessed May 3, 2020).

25. G. Thunberg, "'Our House is on Fire': Greta Thunberg, 16, Urges Leaders to Act on Climate," *The Guardian*, January 25, 2019, https://www.theguardian.com/environment/2019/jan/25/our-house-is-on-fire-greta-thunberg16-urges-leaders-to-act-on-climate (accessed May 3, 2020).

gling in the birth canal. It has no cultural models, no stories of heroes to draw from to inspire hope in a successful outcome. Instead, there is the bare and simple will to live at all costs. There is no calculation of the odds of success, no dependence on imagined outcome, and therefore no hope in the traditional sense of the word. Life simply asserts its intrinsic, unmediated, and absolute value against the onslaught of the powers of death.

This is precisely what seems to have galvanized the meteoric rise of the Extinction Rebellion movement (XR), which has unfolded both in parallel and in concert with the global youth climate protests. Beginning with a handful of academics in the UK in the Fall of 2018, within six months XR had become a growing direct action network spanning more than thirty-five countries. The name of the movement captures perfectly the unconditional visceral affirmation at the heart of the death-rebirth struggle of BPM III, as does its most iconic slogan: "Rebel for Life!". In an article on XR in *The Nation*, Ben Ehrenreich asks the question: "What could it mean to 'act now,' when we have so little time? How to find the will to fight when everything seems doomed?"

> When I asked Clare Farrell, another founding XR organizer, how she managed to keep afloat despite the ever-rising tide of apocalyptic news, she answered by recalling an early XR slogan: "Hope dies, action begins."

> "We act, in other words, on the terrain of hopelessness, and by acting we transform the terrain. Faith is not about belief. It's a leap into action—despite it all, for each other, and for a future that we cannot yet see. Anyway, Farrell said, "to not act is surely hopeless." So we might as well fight while we can."[26]

26. B. Ehrenreich, "There's Only One Antidote for Climate Despair—Climate

Considering the total field of collective consciousness, perhaps it is the case that certain individuals or communities are tasked at any given time with carrying the full weight of one or the other of the Basic Perinatal Matrices, each of which has both negative and positive potentials. Without adequate resources for processing powerful emotions, some will be tragically mired in the bottomless despair of BPM II, while others will be caught up in the heroic deeds of the death-rebirth struggle, the great rebellion for Life (BPM III). Of course it is equally possible that, under the right (or rather, wrong) conditions, the titanic energies associated with BPM III could manifest through acts of domination or malignant aggression, guided not by conscious alignment with the principle of Life as mutual dependence, but on the bare assertion of the will to power. Yet others will be lured into regressive fantasies of miraculous escape into various forms of utopia (BPM I). Again, I will comment on the positive potentials of BPM I (and BPM II) below.

Given what we know of the dynamics of initiation in the context of the birth process, however, it's reasonable to assume that, short of some kind of miraculous delivery on the analogy of an emergency C-section—whether from the advent of the Singularity or takeover from benevolent aliens—some individuals (and perhaps a critical threshold number of them) will need to engage and integrate the complete perinatal gestalt. Having abandoned false hope and yet resolved to labor unconditionally on the side of Life, such individuals and their communities can be seen as preparing the ground for more authentic experiences of BPM IV, which here would correspond to natural delivery in the birth process.

Revolt," *The Nation*. September 9, 2019, https://www.thenation.com/article/extinction-rebellion/ (accessed May 3, 2020).

The Death-Rebirth Experience

As with the other matrices, BPM IV has many typical experiential and symbolic correlates. Its central and defining feature, however, Grof calls *the death-rebirth experience*. Following the (sometimes literal) NDE of labor, this experience involves "the feeling of impending catastrophe of enormous proportions." "If allowed to happen," he continues,

> the transition from BPM III to BPM IV involves the sense of total annihilation on all imaginable levels–physical destruction, emotional disaster, intellectual and philosophical defeat, ultimate moral failure, and absolute damnation of transcendental proportions. This experience of *ego death* seems to entail an instant merciless destruction of all previous reference points in the life of the individual.[27]

Now it's one thing for individuals to undergo this kind of ego death intentionally in the context of personal deep experiential work, as happens in both psychedelic and holotropic therapy, for instance. While the same archetypal dynamics are at play, here it is a case of a new, supraordinate, planetary identity struggling to emerge. In the labor of this transformation, the potential for literal apocalypse is a very real threat that grows with each passing day. The accelerating mass extinction of species, though only now entering the collective consciousness, signals the end of the sixty-six million year Cenozoic era and thus represents the destruction of what has been a fundamental geological baseline since the age of the dinosaurs. More obvious now is the destruction of a stable climate, of reliable seasons, the new normal of extreme

27. Grof, *The Adventure of Self-Discovery*, 30.

weather and climate chaos, and increasing indications of civilizational collapse. With respect to the new planetary identity struggling to emerge, regardless of whether or not humans will succeed in slowing, stopping, or reversing the accelerating catastrophe, it would appear that the new being will not be fully birthed unless or until enough of the old has died. Again we have the central paradox of initiation and the perinatal process that informs it, but now being played out on a planetary scale.

"When experienced in its final and most complete form," writes Grof, "the ego death means an irreversible end to one's philosophical identification with what Alan Watts called [the] *skin-encapsulated ego*."[28] The collective correlate to this ego includes a cluster of related dominant values which continue to structure social relations and the relation of humans to the rest of the Earth community. In Chapter 3 I identified patriarchy, global capitalism, and the more overarching notion of Empire as the main carriers of these values. In Korten's formulation, it will be recalled, Empire is based on

> the hierarchical ordering of human relationships [among humans and between humans and other than humans] based on the principle of domination. The mentality of Empire embraces material excess for the ruling classes, honors the dominator power of death and violence, denies the feminine principle, and suppresses the realization of the potentials of human [and, I would add, other than human] maturity.[29]

Perhaps it is no more than a pipe dream to imagine a world that has been completely liberated from all relations of domination. Still, it is possible to imagine indi-

28. Ibid.
29. Korten, *The Great Turning*, 20.

viduals and communities committed to this liberation, however imperfectly it might be realized. For the new being struggling to emerge—the new Gaianthropic identity in the making—not to end in stillbirth, however, enough individuals and their communities will need to experience the initiatory ego death. Given the persisting dominance of patriarchy and the latter's deep collusion with capitalism and its active role in bringing about the "death of nature,"[30] this is especially true of those strongly (and generally unconsciously) identified with the male value sphere, regardless of whether or not they are cisgender males. It is with these associations in mind that Tarnas wrote, in the concluding lines of *The Passion of the Western Mind*, that "the masculine must undergo a sacrifice, an ego death."[31] In Tarnas's vision, this sacrifice is in the service of a deeper evolutionary telos, a sacred marriage (*hieros gamos*) of archetypal forces, which, in the historical period, and especially since the modern period or Planetary Era, have passed from a phase of differentiation to one of pathological dissociation.[32] "The driving impulse of the West's masculine consciousness," writes Tarnas, "has been its dialectical quest not only to realize itself, but also, finally, to recover its connection with the whole, to come to terms with the great feminine principle in life: to differentiate itself from but then rediscover and reunite with the feminine, with the mystery of life, of nature, of soul."[33]

Clearly, for the sacrifice of the masculine to have any real meaning would require further progress in the liberation of women from oppression of all kinds, an

---

30. See Merchant, *The Death of Nature.*
31. R. Tarnas, *The Passion of the Western Mind: Understanding the Ideas That Have Shaped Our World View* (New York: Harmony Books, 1991), 444.
32. As discussed in Chapters 3 and 4.
33. Ibid., 443.

uprooting of global capitalism, and a generalized resistance to the forces of Empire. Since we can expect both entrenchment and intensified suppression on the part of the ruling patriarchal and capitalist elite, there can be no sacrifice of the masculine without continued striving by those on the side of life. Once again we see the complex character of planetary initiation, where multiple phases of the perinatal process are simultaneously at play: activists engaged in a life and death struggle (BPM III) even as they affirm and seek to embody a life-sustaining worldview (BPM IV) as an alternative to the still reigning values of (patriarchal and capitalist) industrial growth society.

The New Being

Alongside the struggle, and indeed to sustain the struggle, there is a vital need for experiential communion with the life- and meaning-giving ground of individual existence, with what we might call the Gaian and cosmic womb of interbeing. For most people such communion is not possible without some kind of regular contact with the other-than-human world, whether something as simple (though shockingly rare for much of the world's increasingly urban population) as witnessing a sunrise or sunset, being under the stars at night, walking through woods, or sitting by a stream. Though intrinsically healing, the impact of such contact is greatly amplified when met with the appropriate psychic attitude. In terms of perinatal dynamics or the death-rebirth archetype, there must be a wholesome relation to BPM I, whose archetypal virtues can serve, as James writes in a different context, as a kind of "mystical bath and refuge for feeling when tired Reason sickens of her intellectual responsibilities."[34] For all indigenous, and indeed all premodern,

34. W. James, "On Some Hegelisms," in *William James: Writings 1878–1899*, ed.

cultures, where intellect had not yet been divorced from the archetypal imagination, Earth was seen, as Thomas Berry puts it, not as a mere collection of objects, but rather as a communion of subjects. It is in this light that we can understand the many calls for some time now for a "re-enchantment of the world." Along with the growing interest in indigenous spiritualities, one can point to several trends in academic discourse, which, to varying degrees, seek to reinstate the idea of the *anima mundi*— that Earth has a soul—including in such fields as Jungian, archetypal,[35]and transpersonal psychology; ecofeminist spirituality; deep, spiritual, and integral ecologies; and even the revival of panpsychism in contemporary philosophical and scientific circles. "What seems to be unfolding," as Tarnas remarked in his 2001 essay,

> is not only a recovery of the anima mundi but a new relationship to it. Something new is being forged; it is not simply a "regression" to a premodern state. We seem to be moving to a world view that is a dialectical synthesis of world and self, a new vision of the universe reflected in the many scientific and philosophical impulses working today toward a participatory holistic paradigm.[36]

We have seen that, under stress of the initiatory crisis, there is the danger of less wholesome retreat or regression to the amniotic security of BPM I, whether through mere intoxication or through soothing fantasies of all kinds. Or there is fixation on the promise of miraculous delivery (BPM IV) as distraction from the struggles at hand. In a successful initiation, by contrast, a renewed and wholesome relation to the nurturing archetypal po-

G.E. Meyers (New York: Library of America, 1992), 661.

35. See, in this connection, James Hillman's seminal essay, "Anima mundi: The return of the soul to the world." *Spring* (1982): 71–93.

36. Tarnas, "Is the Modern Psyche Undergoing a Rite of Passage?", 21.

tentials of BPM I is granted as a boon to the newly forged identity (often marked by feasting and celebration of the successful initiate). With regard to the perinatal process as engaged in actual birth, the ego death that marks the transition from BPM III to BPM IV is followed, ideally at least, with the nurturing of the body and being of the neonate, who, though absolutely dependent on the maternal organism or primary care giver, is now a relatively autonomous biological and psychosocial individual. As with its body relative to the body of the "mother," the ego of the neonate is nevertheless initially given to (and in need of) periodic fusion with the archetypal matrix out of which it has just emerged. As with the body, this fusion doubtless sustains and vitalizes the fledgling ego, needing to be fed, as it were, by a kind of psychic mother's milk.

Though repeating some of the same dynamics as in the case of the neonate, the new Gaianthropic identity that seems to be luring the planetary initiation underway includes new layers of complexity. This should not be surprising, given that this initiation involves adults rather than neonates. It is also collective and even planetary rather merely individual, even if the new identity is only actual insofar as it lives in individuals. The complexity manifests as a second paradox (the first, core paradox, it will be recalled, is that birth equals death), this time inhering in the relation between the two constitutive terms of the new identity: *Gaia* and *Anthropos*. In the case of individual birth, the neonate comes into the world in a state of absolute dependence on the maternal organism (for food, warmth, protection, etc.). In the case of the current planetary initiation, the human retains a state of absolute dependence on Gaia as the greater maternal (super)organism. A distinguishing feature of the Anthropocene/Gaianthropocene, however, is a new state of dependence of Gaian systems (atmosphere, hydrosphere, pedosphere, biosphere) on the human for their continued integrity. In this sense, Gaia takes on some, at least, of the role of the neonate, while the human takes on some of the role of the maternal organism or primary care giver. The new relation of dependence is perhaps not absolute insofar as these systems could presumably survive human extinction. Nevertheless, human actions in the short-term will be the primary factor in determining future levels of biodiversity and the ecological resilience of these systems on geological time-scales. In this sense, humans depend upon Gaia, who now also depends on us.[37]

Conclusion

Returning to the tension between those commit-ted to the need for hope for the successful transition to an ecological civilization, on the one hand, and those convinced of the inevitability of collapse, on the other, we can conclude with the following observations. Wheth-er by temperament or by virtue of other conditioning factors, individuals will be particularly sensitive to the archetypal constellations associated with one or the other of the perinatal matrices (or meta-matrices). One should honor these sensitivities, raise them to consciousness, and devote them to the common cause of the planetary initiation underway. Both camps can be, and generally are, united in the struggle for the sake of life (BPM III).

37. In terms of the principles of complexity articulated by Edgar Morin and ex-plored in Chapter 4, we could say that the relation between Gaia and Anthropos is at once recursive, dialogical, and holographic (that is, in a state of dynamic tension, each term both contains/generates and is contained/generated by the other). We see this complex/paradoxical relation intuited and expressed mytho-poetically in the series of rituals devoted to Pachamama, the Incan Earth-Mother goddess, and especially in the central ritual of *Challa*, the root meaning of which is "to feed and to give drink to the land." For a description of one such ritual in modern day Bolivia, which includes not only herbs and sweets, but the traditional llama fetus as part of the offering, see: J. Ingham, "Bolivia's offerings to Mother Earth," *BBC News*, October 28, 2007, http://news.bbc.co.uk/2/hi/pro-grammes/from_our_own_correspondent/7062647.stm (accessed May 3, 2020).

Those drawn to hope need to be wary of eliding feelings of pain, constriction, sadness, and despair (BPM II), honoring them, as Joanna Macy reminds us to do,[38] as natural expressions of a deeper love for the world. Those convinced of the inevitability of collapse, and thus more prone to potentially debilitating despair, would benefit through acknowledging the restorative and generative potentials of imagining positive or even ideal futures (BPM I and BPM IV), even as they relinquish attachment to any specific outcome. The main task for both would be to embody as much as possible the complete perinatal gestalt, affirming their shared commitment to the goal of liberation (BPM IV), lured by the same Gaianthropic identity in the making.

"Are we going to make it?", Tarnas asked at the turn of the new millennium.

> We cannot be completely sure that we will. No authentic initiatory process begins in the certainty of its outcome. It is not at all certain that we will successfully pass through this eye of the needle, this planetary ego death. For the foreseeable future, we seem to be living in an era of high drama. We seem to be engaged now in a kind of race...between initiation and catastrophe.[39]

The intervening decades have only intensified the drama. While I, for one, have come to accept the inevitability of civilizational collapse, I still have faith in the process of initiation. The nature of this faith is explored in the following chapter.

---

38. See J. Macy, *World as Lover, World as Self: Courage for Global Justice and Ecological Renewal* (Berkeley: Parallax Press, 2007); and S. Kelly and J. Macy, "The Great Turning: Reconnecting Through Collapse," in *Deep Adaptation: Pathways through Climate Chaos*, eds. J. Bendell and R. Read (forthcoming).

39. Tarnas, "Is the Modern Psyche Undergoing a Rite of Passage?", 23.

6

Living in End Times: Beyond Hope and Despair

The nightworld is where we are.
I say it. I say it till we may hear it.
And in that darkness, we remember what we love the most.
That itself is the candle.
—Martin Shaw

Those I wish to reach

Even in the time since I began writing these pages, more and more people I encounter have fallen into a deepening despair. Others have proposed revisions to the traditional meaning of hope, revisions that are not dependent upon the expectation of a successful outcome. These proposals, some of my friends and colleagues feel, are essential not only to prevent sinking further into despair, but to encourage the kind of activism we so need if, indeed, there is still a fighting chance to avoid the worst. I respect these proposals, even if I am no longer able to ground myself in them. This chapter, therefore, is especially for those who, consciously or unconsciously, have already abandoned all hope that we will be able to prevent civilizational collapse and completely halt the accelerating Great Unraveling. There are many too whose heart-mind lives in a divided state, caught in a distressing oscillation between despair and hope, and who might benefit from a creative, third way. As an alternative to hope, however it might be defined, I explore the possibility of a new kind of faith, a faith grounded in the experience of wisdom and the affirmation of love. Rooted in this ground, I suggest that we might find a way to live in these end times beyond both hope and despair, a way that makes room for grief, fear, even anger, but also for joy, delight, and a deep sense of meaning and purpose.

Let me be clear: Though I am seeking to cultivate a path beyond both hope and despair when it comes to the fate of industrial civilization or the possibility of saving the biological diversity that humans have always enjoyed throughout our brief sojourn in Gaia, I do honor the value of hope for a better future in place of a worse one which is always possible. Whatever the challenges we will be facing, we can always choose the better course. We can celebrate and amplify the light, however over-whelming the darkness might seem. In the end, however, I believe that even this more modest hope for a better world, rather than an ideal best of all worlds, can only be sustained if grounded in the new kind of faith explored later in this chapter.

In what follows, I begin with the idea that we live in end times. After considering some recent attempts to redefine or limit the meaning of the word hope, I go on to explore resonances between our personal mortality and the planetary initiation that we are being drawn into, an initiation, as we have seen in previous chapters, that is constellating a collective near-death experience. For the rest of the chapter, I circle around a series of intimations of what it might mean to waken in these end times to our deeper, more integral selves. Here I focus on how experience of what I call *integral time* reveals the intrinsic, and indeed infinite, value of the actions we might still take on behalf of Gaia and the entire web of life, in whatever time we have left.

Living in End Times

We live in end times. "But there have always been end times!" I have heard people say in reply. I imagine someone elaborating further: "Ancient empires fell, replaced by others that fell in their turn. Civilizations, cultures, families and their names, languages, cities, alliances, friendships, marriages, countless individual lives, countless species even have all passed away, and their worlds with them, in the ever-flowing river of time. Everything passes, yes, but every end is merely a transition to a new beginning. How many times have seers and prophets, especially near the ends or beginning of centuries or millennia, proclaimed, 'the End is nigh!', their voices inevitably fading into the relentless sweep of history and the ceaseless rhythm of daily life?"

I am no prophet, but I have come to accept that we do in fact live in end times. The 12,000 year period known as the Holocene, which began once the great ice sheets retreated far enough that, in time, and given the stable and favorable global climate, the agricultural revolution could begin, has come to an end. The Anthropocene, which the scientific and most of the academic community have agreed to call the geological epoch now upon us, also signals the end of the much longer 66,000,000 year Cenozoic Era that began with the extinction of the dinosaurs (which were among the 76% of the world's species that went extinct). The current mass extinction now well underway is occurring at a faster rate than the one that took out the dinosaurs. The time between these two mass extinctions is almost unimaginably long. The vast majority of mammalian species that preceded the emergence of humans (the youngest among the mammals) evolved during the Cenozoic. They are going extinct at 1,000 to 10,000 times the normal rate and it now seems increasingly likely that more than half of all known species (not just mammals) will be gone forever in a little more than a decade. The reality of our moment is that the world as humans have always experienced it, and even as most mammals experienced it long before the emergence of humans, is coming to an end in real time, this time.

Again, some might say at this point, as many of my friends and colleagues do, "But it's still not too late! The Earth system is so complex, and in all complex systems there is radical uncertainty and the possibility of sudden phase shifts, of creative, emergent properties that can't be foreseen before the event. We have the technological means and practical know-how to transition out of the mess we're in. We can halt the plunge into climate chaos and even regenerate the natural systems upon which we depend. We can do this, and we will because we must!" I find this kind of response unconvincing, however, in the face of compelling (and increasingly dire) scientific reports combined with the realities of the political economy.[1] Granted the fact of irreducible uncertainty, in the light of all available evidence, my assessment of the probability of success comes to resemble the chances of winning a weekly lottery. Even if I am literally betting

1. There are too many relevant studies to cite here, and doubtless more are to come. For a recent treatment of our planetary emergency that draws from many of the most relevant from the last few years, even if I do not agree with his conclusions, see D. Wallace-Wells, *The Uninhabitable Earth: Life After Warming* (New York: Tim Duggan Books, 2019). See also D. Jamail's regular columns in Truthout.org, which have links to relevant studies. See also J. Bendell, "Deep Adaptation: A Map for Navigating Climate Tragedy," Institute of Leadership and Sustainability, July 27, 2018, https://www.lifeworth.com/deepadaptation.pdf (accessed May 3, 2020). I also recommend Catherine Ingram's courageous essay, "Facing Extinction" which, after presenting hyperlinked summaries of many of the most recent studies, offers wise counsel on living in end times from her own deep engagement with the Buddha Dharma. C. Ingram, "Facing Extinction," March 2020, http://www.catherineingram.com/facingextinction/ (accessed May 3, 2020). Finally, see Pablo Servigne and Raphaël Stevens, *How Everything Can Collapse* (Cambridge: Polity Press, 2020).

on winning by buying a ticket, I know in my heart that this is an indulgence and that I cannot reasonably expect to win. I realize that the planetary emergency we find ourselves in is orders of magnitude more complex than the largest of lotteries and that it is not a question of passively submitting ourselves to overwhelming odds. I also acknowledge that opinion is divided among the most informed communities as to whether or not we have already passed the point of no return in our plunge toward catastrophe. Finally, there are many very intelligent and passionate people (some my close friends) who believe that, especially in light of such overwhelming odds, it is more than ever necessary to embrace some kind of hope. Otherwise, they feel, we risk losing whatever little moral or emotional ground we have left to stand on. Again, it is not my intention to persuade these people to abandon their last stand. For my part, regardless of the possibility or probability of a successful outcome, I maintain that nothing should come in the way of doing everything in our power to avoid the worst, or more positively stated, to secure the achievable. At the same time, I want to be as honest as I can be in face of our current situation. For now, at least, for my own benefit and for those either caught in despair or dissatisfied with a divided heart-mind, I want to explore a creative alternative to hope, even in its most "active" or "radical" forms.

On the Meaning and Emptying of the Word Hope

A standard definition of the word "hope" includes the following (from the *Cambridge Dictionary*):

1. the feeling that something desired **can be had or will** happen
2. to express the **feeling or wish** that something desired will happen
3. to **want** something to happen or to be true, and

usually **have a good reason to think that it might**
4. something good that **you want** to happen in the
future, or a **confident feeling** about what will happen in
the future

I certainly have no issues with #2, and I use the word
all the time in this sense, as when I say, "I hope it won't
rain tomorrow" or "I hope he gets here soon!". But there
also are many things I might want or wish would happen, but in my heart I know or at least strongly suspect
that they will not come to pass, as in the case of betting
in the lottery mentioned above. A more serious example
would be when visiting an emaciated friend in hospital
following a terminal diagnosis. One might wish or pray
for a miraculous cure, a late-term spontaneous remission,
but our heart or gut tells us to prepare for the worst.
The question then becomes, What grounds are there for
holding to #1 ("can be had or will happen"), #3 ("have
a good reason to think that it might"), or #4 (a confident
feeling about the future")? While even just a few years
ago I was able to affirm, however tentatively, #1, #3, or
#4, if I am honest with myself I must admit that I see
no grounds for using the word hope in connection with
our planetary emergency. It is under the weight of this
realization, even if not always fully integrated, that many
people are trying to revision the meaning of "hope", as
with the phrase "radical hope" or "active hope."[2]

2. A similar wave of new thinking around hope arose in Christian circles the
1960s with various expressions of the "theology of hope." Associated with the
writings of Ernst Bloch, Johannes Metz, Wolfgang Pannenberg, Karl Rahner, and
especially Jürgen Moltmann, these theologies of hope draw on the eschatological faith in the return of Christ and the promise of a "New Heaven and New
Earth" as ground for transformative action in the here and now. As Moltmann
put it in 1993: "Those who hope in Christ can no longer put up with reality as it
is, but begin to suffer under it, to contradict it. Peace with God means conflict
with the world, for the goad of the promised future stabs inexorably into the
flesh of every unfulfilled present." This kind of hope "makes the Church the

I remember well, during the first few years of co-teaching the course, "The Great Turning", with Joanna Macy at the California Institute of Integral Studies (CIIS), how she would sometimes bristle at the word "hope." Influenced by her deep engagement in the Buddha Dharma ("the word 'hope' does not figure in Buddhist texts," Joanna[3] has reminded me on several occasions) and no doubt by her rejection of the other-worldly dimension of her childhood Christianity (though she has retained a deep respect for many other elements of the Christian tradition), Joanna considered much talk of hope a distraction from giving our full attention and commitment to our present predicament. Then, to my surprise, in 2012, Joanna (with Chris Johnstone) pro-posed the idea of "active hope" as a strategy for "facing the mess we're in without going crazy" (which is the subtitle of their co-authored book, *Active Hope*). Here is how they defined the term:

> Passive hope is about waiting for external agencies to bring about what we desire. Active Hope is about becoming active participants in bringing about what we hope for.

source of continual new impulses towards the realization of righteousness, freedom and humanity here in the light of the promised future that is to come" (quoted in Stephen Brown, "50 years after Theology of Hope, Jürgen Molt-mann's vision continues to inspire," in *World Council of Churches*, 03 February 2016: https://www.oikoumene.org/news/50-years-after-theology-of-hope-jur-gen-moltmanns-vision-continues-to-inspire#_ftn2: accessed October 21, 2020). While many believing Christians might still be able to affirm such a theology of hope, most contemporary revisionings of the meaning of hope fall outside formal theological circles, Christian or otherwise. In the absence of the eschato-logical faith which might ground this kind of hope, the more secular revisions, to my mind, are largely stop-gap measures and, for a growing portion of the population, may not provide a solid enough foundation for the kind of activism and engagement called for in these end times.

3. As it feels awkward for me always to refer to friends by their full or last names, after the first mention I will use only their first names.

Active Hope is a practice. Like tai chi or gardening, it is something we *do* rather than *have*. It is a process we can apply to any situation, and it involves three key steps. First, we take a clear view of reality; second, we identify what we hope for in terms of the direction we'd like things to move in or the values we'd like to see expressed; and third, we take steps to move ourselves or our situation in that direction.

Since Active Hope doesn't require our optimism, we can apply it even in areas where we feel hopeless. The guiding impetus is intention; we *choose* what we aim to bring about, act for, or express. Rather than weighing our chances and proceeding only when we feel hopeful, we focus on our *intention* and let it be our guide.[4]

I worked with this understanding of hope for a few years, during which time I still believed we had fighting chance of achieving the Great Turning toward a life-sustaining civilization. While I remain as committed as ever to the fundamental values that inform the idea of the Great Turning—at the center of which is a view of the human as embedded within, and called to protect and celebrate, the web of life and wider Earth community—I can no longer in good faith hold to any expectation that we will halt the accelerating Great Unravelling or Great Dying, as others call it. Despite this lack of expectation, this absence of hope, I am also just as committed to enacting the three dimensions of the Great Turning that Joanna has identified: *holding actions* to slow, if not halt, the unraveling; promotion of *Gaian structures* as life-affirming alternatives to the ways of business as usual; and the *shift in consciousness* associated with the growing

4. J. Macy and C. Johnstone, *Active Hope: How to Face the Mess We're in without Going Crazy* (New World Library, 2012), 3.

awareness of our deeper Gaian identity and our inter-being with all that is.

A question naturally arises at this point: If you really believe that these are end times, that we will in all likelihood not be able to halt the Great Unraveling, where is the motivation to keep fighting on the side of life? Even while still accepting the theoretical principle of radical uncertainty, if collapse and mass extinction seem increasingly inevitable, how might we muster the strength, or why even bother trying, to slow down or "mitigate" the approaching catastrophe?[5] For a while, I approached this question with the following, admittedly extreme, analogy: You are walking along an ocean beach as a massive storm approaches and you see three people in a row get

---

5. Philosopher Lajos Brons has this to say, commenting on S. Scheffler's 2013 book, *Death and the Afterlife*:

> As Samuel Scheffler has forcefully argued, "the actual value of our activities depends on their place in an ongoing human history" and "humanity itself as an ongoing historical project provides the implicit frame of reference for most of our judgments about what matters" (p. 54 and 60, respectively). Scheffler argues convincingly that in a doomed or dying world "people would lose confidence in the value of many sorts of activities, would cease to see reason to engage in many familiar sorts of pursuits, and would become emotionally detached from many of those activities and pursuits" (p. 44).
>
> What's the point of writing a book or article, or composing a piece of music, if civilization is collapsing? A few people might read it or listen to it in the next couple of decades, but before the end of the century it will almost certainly be lost. What's the point of raising and educating children if their education only prepares them for a society that will collapse at some point during their lifetime, and if they are likely to be subjected to (neofascist) repression, violence, war, and poverty? It's not difficult to give other examples. The point is that without a future, very little matters. Without a future for mankind, almost everything that matters to us loses its value. It is for this reason that Scheffler asserts that "the collective afterlife [i.e. the survival of mankind] matters more to people than the personal afterlife" (p. 72).

L. Brons, "Fictionalism – or: Vaihinger, Scheffler, and Kübler-Ross at the End of the World," *F=ma*, October 22, 2018, http://www.lajosbrons.net/blog/fictionalism-about-the-future/ (accessed May 3, 2020).

pulled out to sea by a powerful rip tide and quickly go under. Your child had just then let go of your hand for a moment and run to the surf's edge and she too is taken by a crashing wave. Someone beside you tries to hold you back as you see your child calling out, struggling not to be pulled under as she is carried quickly away. I imagine you, like most parents, would jump into the water to try and save their child, regardless of risk or the apparent chances of success. Why is this the case?

The same question could be asked in the not uncommon situation of someone responding altruistically and with great risk to themselves to the distress of a total stranger. In both cases there appears to be an immediate empathic identification with the other, which of course is not too surprising with a parent and their child and is understandably lauded in cases of altruism. Though not the result of conscious ethical reasoning, such actions seem to involve a spontaneous, non-reflective affirmation of the value of a life, and more, of human life itself as something that transcends one's individual claim to it. Reasoning after the fact, we could say that this affirmation involves the intuition that certain things are intrinsically right and good, regardless of how likely they are to succeed, how long they might last, or however imperfectly they might be realized.

In the case of parents and children, it is a common assumption that parents ought to love their children unconditionally. We also know the devastating effects conditional love can have on the development of a child's sense of core identity. As adults as well, we all crave unconditional love. Imagine someone who told or showed you that they would love you, if and only if you could succeed at certain tasks they put before you. Even if you satisfied their demands, you would not experience the kind of love you most craved. As with love, so it is for all the things we truly value as good and worthwhile.

Bringing this back to the matter at hand, I am re-minded of a close friend and colleague, now in her late eighties, who confided in me recently that she has been caught between feelings of deep grief and numbness at the prospect of the unraveling of complex life. The numbness sometimes takes the form of a sense of meaninglessness. After all, how can one have a sense of meaning in life if life itself as humans have always experienced it seems to be coming to an end? I asked her the following question, which I often pose to myself when beset by these same feelings: "Would you feel any different if you knew with certainty that life in all its richness would continue for another several billions of years? If so, what about fifty million? What about a thousand years?" "I see where you're going with this," she said with a wry smile. My intention, of course, was to perform a similar move to Zeno's paradox of Achilles and the hare. Instead of trying to argue for the illusory character of motion, however, in this case my intention was to arrive at the realization and affirmation of the intrinsic value, in a sense the infinite value, of finite time, even if this amounts to just a day, an hour, this next moment…. Because the value is intrinsic, it—or the things which embody it (love, compassion, justice, life itself) call out to be affirmed, protected, ampli-fied, cherished, and celebrated unconditionally.

Vaclav Havel appeals to this intuition of intrinsic value, even if I am not able to follow him in using it to redefine the meaning of hope. In his own "active" or "radical" recasting of the word, hope

> is not the same as joy that things are going well, or willingness to invest in enterprises that are obviously headed for early success, but rather an ability to work for something *because it is good*, not just because it stands a chance to succeed. The more unpromising the situation in which we demonstrate hope, the deeper

that hope is. Hope is not the same thing as optimism. It is not the conviction that something will turn out well, but the certainty that *something makes sense, regardless of how it turns out.*[6]

This kind of hope, writes Havel, "is not prognostication." He continues:

It is an orientation of the spirit, an orientation of the heart. It transcends the world that is immediately experienced, and is anchored somewhere beyond its horizons.... I feel that its deepest roots are in the transcendental, just as the roots of human responsibility are, though of course I can't – unlike Christians, for instance—say anything about the transcendental...[7]

I don't think, however, that we can or should avoid talking about the "transcendental." Though Havel distinguishes his position from that of most Christians, in his reference to "somewhere beyond its horizons" he would seem to be searching for a substitute for the Christian eschatological orientation in the absence of the faith position that made this orientation possible. Despite the early Christian and continuing, if countercultural, tradition of a more "realized eschatology" that stresses the immanent saving power of faith in Christ, the dominant faith position maintained the belief that this world is a "vale of tears" and that ultimate salvation would come only after the end times (*eschaton*). "And if our hope in Christ is only for this life," as Paul wrote to the Corinthians, "we are more to be pitied than anyone in the

---

6. V. Havel, *Disturbing the Peace: A Conversation with Karel Huizdala* (New York: Vintage Books, 1991), 181-182. My italics.

7. Ibid.

world."[8] Though Christians believed that it was possible, whether through the grace of faith alone or through the sacraments, to enjoy a provisional or anticipatory kind of salvation while awaiting the final judgment, Christian hope was one of a confident expectation (sense #4 above) of the blessedness of eternal life, not of the ultimate over-coming of evil in this life. This is not to deny, however, that many Christians have and are still committed to confronting evil in this life, or that their sense of hope is not a significant factor in such commitment.[9]

With the emergence in modern times of the Enlight-enment ideal of endless progress and belief in the perfect-ibility of the human, it was possible, having lost the earli-er faith, to cultivate a confidence (*con-fides*, "with faith") in this-worldly salvation. This second kind of faith, how-ever, was shaken to the core by the horrors of the two world wars. The twentieth century came to be under-

---

8. I *Corinthians*, 15:19.

9. In his *Passion of the Western Mind*, Richard Tarnas encapsulates the realized eschatology of what he terms "exultant Christianity" (in contrast to what became the dominant "dualistic" stream) as follows: "Here an unprecedented cosmic optimism was asserted. In its physicality and historicity, Christ's resurrection held forth the promise that everything—all history both of individuals and of mankind, all striving, all mistakes and sins and imperfections, all materiality, the entire drama and reality of Earth—would somehow be swept up and perfected in a final victorious reunion with the infinite Godhead.... While they eagerly anticipated Christ's Second Coming, the Parousia ('Presence'), when he would return from the heavens in full glory before the entire world, their awareness was centered on the liberating fact that Christ had already initiated the redemptive process—a triumphant process in which they could directly participate. On this basis was constituted the overriding Christian attitude of hope. Through the Christian faithful's continuing act of hope in God's compassionate power and plan for humanity, the trials and terrors of the present world could be tran-scended. Humanity could now look forward, in humble confidence, to a glorious future fulfillment which its own attitude of hope was in some way helping to real-ize." (127, 128) As Tarnas makes clear, though expressive of a profound sense of liberation in the present, this faith position was nevertheless grounded in a confident expectation of "the glorious future fulfillment" of the Second Coming.

stood by many as the "age of anxiety,"[10] and this despite
the sense among the allies at least of having triumphed
over evil. It is true that Soviet and Chinese communism
managed for a while to maintain faith in this-worldly
salvation, and that the North Atlantic civilization of the
60s and early 70s in particular could point to remarkable
accomplishments in many areas—including advances in
science, technology, and material well-being, as well as
in democracy and human rights. Such accomplishments
could counter the growing sense throughout the Cold War
of potential nuclear apocalypse and, however provisionally, bolster the early modern faith in human progress. The
already shaky ground of this secular faith, however, has
finally completely given way with the reality of runaway
climate chaos and the accelerating mass extinction, both
of which had not entered the collective consciousness at
the time Havel was writing (1991).

While the word hope may be stretched too thin to
serve, Havel is right, I feel, in invoking a "transcendental" orientation of the spirit and the heart. What are the
possibilities available to us, in these end times, in trying
to cultivate such an orientation?

Planetary Initiation

As we saw in the previous chapter, for the past two
decades a few of my colleagues and I have been character-
izing our moment as one of being poised on the threshold
of planetary initiation. In all traditional societies, major
life transitions (puberty, grave illness, becoming a tribal
leader) are marked by rites of passage or initiation, the
purpose of which is to deconstruct an old identity and

---

10. See F. Le Van Baumer, *Main Currents Of Western Thought: Readings In Western Europe Intellectual History From The Middle Ages To The Present* (New Haven:
Yale UP, 1978), 647ff.

summon a new one. In our case, it will be recalled, the initiation is planetary not only in the sense that it involves all members (and species) of the Earth community, but also in that the new human identity being called into being is itself planetary, or Gaian, in character. We now have detailed knowledge of our species as an expression of the 4.6 billion years unfolding of Earth evolution. And while our times mark the beginning of the Anthropocene, or Gaianthropocene, which involves a recognition of the degree to which the human has become a geological force in its own right, these times also coincide with the growing awareness of how intimately, how inextricably, our fate is tied to that of the web of life and other Gaian systems in which we are embedded. In even stronger terms, the new, planetary identity in the making is not only a question of human transformation. Earth or Gaia herself is waking up to herself through this human transformation, but in some sense transcending the human as well. In any case, as in many traditional rites of passage, the planetary initiation underway seems to involve and even require a confrontation with death. However we might measure the success of the initiation, it cannot proceed without some kind of death, or at least without some kind of near death experience (NDE). The important point for now is the idea that we are being swept up in an archetypal process of transformation that is inherently spiritual or "transcendental" in nature. Though we have no certain vision as to outcome, we know from the nature of the archetypal process involved that avoiding, denying, or otherwise diluting the full force of the planetary NDE being constellated risks aborting the new identity struggling to be born.

Terminal Diagnosis

Zhiwa Woodbury was perhaps the first to apply an (eco)psychospiritual understanding of how individuals respond to a terminal diagnosis to the growing collective consciousness of these end times. In line with the importance that Joanna has assigned to "honoring our pain for the world" in the practice of the "Work that Reconnects", Zhiwa suggests that the grief, anger, and fear that more and more people are feeling in connection with the "Anthropogenic Great Dying" is consistent with what we know about the stages of grief associated with the prospect of one's own death. Over the course of about fifty years, writes Woodbury,

> we have gone from: being vaguely aware that something was terribly wrong in our relationship to our mother, Earth; to a phase of denial that, in fact, we are in the midst of a great extinction of species and a threat to continued life on the planet in the face of mounting evidence to that effect; and, finally we have arrived at a time when nobody can credibly pretend anymore that we are not on a disastrous course—it is quite clear that life as we know it is coming to an end. During this same time frame, we have witnessed a progression in the American populace of dramatic increases in the incidence of anxiety disorders at the start, then widespread depression, and more recently, mass murder and suicide rates.[11]

Zhiwa asks what a "good death" might look like as we accelerate into what are sure to be ever more chaotic times. Here he draws from both palliative care and hospice work, suggesting how we might adapt them to the growing awareness of the Great Dying. As with assisting individuals to accept and prepare for their individual deaths, Zhiwa imagines the emergence of *planetary hospice* work-

11. Z. Woodbury, "Planetary Hospice: Rebirthing Planet Earth," 18, https://guymcpherson.com/wp-content/uploads/2014/03/Planetary-Hospice.pdf (accessed May 3, 2020).

ers as spiritual midwives who will help "transform the planetary death/ rebirth process from a painful dislocation rife with suffering and regret into a healing process for both the human race and the Earth itself—even into a Great Awakening."[12] My thinking is very much aligned with Zhiwa's creative perspective and his suggestions for how best to prepare for a "good death". He too grounds the deeper meaning of our end times in the archetype of initiation or death/rebirth being played out on a planetary scale. Both of us also stress the need to draw from multiple sources of spiritual wisdom, both ancient and contemporary, to assist us as we straddle the threshold of these end times.

Zhiwa's multi- and transdisciplinary proposal for planetary hospice work is one of the earliest and most powerful proposals, from a psychospiritual perspective, for the kind of *reconciliation* Jem Bendell has recently called for as the fourth "R" in his courageous proposal for "deep adaptation" to our planetary emergency. The first three "R's" are resilience, relinquishment, and restoration: *resilience* involves "the capacity to adapt to changing circumstances so as to survive with valued norms and behaviours"; *relinquishment* involves people and communities "letting go of certain assets, behaviours and beliefs where retaining them could make matters worse"; and *restoration* involves "people and communities rediscovering attitudes and approaches to life and organisation that our hydrocarbon-fueled civilisation eroded."[13] I encourage readers to consult Jem's original paper for particulars on the first three "R's" as well as for his detailed and sobering summary of current climate science, insightful reflections on denial, and more. As

12. Ibid., 10.
13. Bendell, "Deep Adaptation," 23.

for *reconciliation*, Jem is guided by the question, "What could I make peace with to lessen suffering?" This question, he writes,

> incorporates the idea of Reconciliation with one's death, including any difficulties and regrets in one's life, any anger towards existence itself (or God). It also invites reconciliation between peoples, genders, classes, generations, countries, religions and political persuasions. Because it is time to make our peace. Otherwise, without this inner deep adaptation to climate collapse we risk tearing each other apart and dying hellishly. My radical hope is that more of us work together to achieve this reconciliation, in all its forms, as a basis for the fuller deep adaptation agenda...[14]

The Inscription over the Gate

Zhiwa and Jem both retain an appeal to hope. Zhiwa's hope is minimalist in the sense that, while accepting the reality of the Great Dying, he nevertheless holds to a firm belief in the survivability of the human species, a belief which he also feels is necessary to avoid being completely overwhelmed by despair. "The end of life as we know it," he writes, "is not equivalent to humanity's end, and that is a message that needs to be clear."[15] Jem, for his part, works with the formula of "inevitable [civilizational] collapse, probable [ecological] catastrophe, and possible human extinction". This somber assessment is offset by his call for a "radical" hope based on "a highly aspirational, credible and relatable vision." He maintains that ours is a time

14. J. Bendell, "Hope and Vision in the Face of Collapse—The 4th R of Deep Adaptation," January 9, 2019, https://jembendell.com/2019/01/09/hope-and-vision-in-the-face-of-collapse-the-4th-r-of-deep-adaptation/ (accessed May 3, 2020).

15. Woodbury, "Planetary Hospice," 22.

to drop all hopes and visions that arise from an inability to accept impermanence and non-control, and instead describe a radical hope of how we respond in these times. I believe it's possible and necessary, through mutual inquiry and support, for our fears, beliefs or certainties of collapse to be brought to a place of peaceful inner and outer resourcefulness. Ours is a time for reconciliation with mortality, nature and each other.[16]

I agree completely that no creative response to these end times is possible unless we find our way to embrace impermanence and befriend mortality. And while I also believe that any satisfying reconciliation with death, whether individual or collective, must involve the kind of spiritual or transcendental perspective invoked by Havel, some of us, at least, will be called to relinquish even this last refuge of hope, however radical it might be.[17]

We will be like Dante before the Gate of Hell. Of course, humans have always known many kinds of hell. Hundreds of millions now live their own version of hell through hunger, violence, and oppression of all kinds. And if this were not enough, the Great Dying already begun and the imminent prospect of civilizational collapse call upon those of us privileged enough to do so to walk unflinchingly through the forbidding Gate, perhaps to

16. Bendell, "Hope and Vision."

17. In his detailed response to what he characterizes as the "green positivity" perspective of Jeremy Lent's critique of the Deep Adaptation agenda, Jem writes that "I have come to see any hope, even radical, as influenced by our egos' fear of the unknown. All hope is a story of the future rather than attention to the present. If we lived 'hopefree' rather than hopeful, might we take more ownership and responsibility for how we are living in the present?" For Jeremy's response to Jem's deep adaptation agenda and for his own proposal for "deep transformation," see J. Lent, "Our Actions Create the Future: A Response to Jem Bendell," Patterns of Meaning, April 11, 2019, https://patternsofmeaning.com/2019/04/11/our-actions-create-the-future-a-response-to-jem-bendell/ (accessed May 3, 2020).

harrow Hell anew as Christ is said to have done between his death and resurrection or, with the Bodhisattva, Jizou, to console those in torment with the promise of liberation. Like Dante, we will need a wise companion (or community) by our side and, Spirit willing, we can anticipate an encounter with our own Beatrice, of whom I shall have more to say below. As we who are called to do so cross the threshold as conscious participants in this new Divine Comedy of planetary initiation, however, we would do well to heed the inscription over the gate:

> THROUGH ME THE WAY INTO THE SUFFERING CITY,
> THROUGH ME THE WAY TO THE ETERNAL PAIN,
> THROUGH ME THE WAY THAT RUNS AMONG THE LOST.
> JUSTICE URGED ON MY HIGH ARTIFICER;
> MY MAKER WAS DIVINE AUTHORITY,
> THE HIGHEST WISDOM, AND THE PRIMAL LOVE.
> BEFORE ME NOTHING BUT ETERNAL THINGS
> WERE MADE, AND I ENDURE ETERNALLY.
> ABANDON EVERY HOPE, WHO ENTER HERE.[18]

Unfinished Business

Before continuing with some reflections of a more explicitly transcendental or spiritual nature, I want to dwell a little longer on the meaning of a "good death" in these end times. It is a common experience for individuals who have come to terms with a terminal diagnosis, having passed the stage of denial and crippling fear, anger, and despair, to be gripped with a vital passion to attend to "unfinished business." While the latter can include un-realized goals or aspirations common to many so-called bucket lists (visiting long dreamed of travel destinations, physically risky adventures, finally attending to a neglected

18. Dante, *Inferno*, Canto 3, lines 1- 9. (Mandelbaum translation): https://digit-aldante.columbia.edu/dante/divine-comedy/inferno/inferno-3/

Figure 1: Dante and
Virgil at the Gate of Hell
(William Blake)

passion, etc.) more typically such business has to do with
making peace with others, and oneself, with seizing this
last opportunity to "make things right." This can take
the form of a confession or other kinds of truth-telling,
of asking for forgiveness, or of finally offering forgiveness to others, and of making amends for harm done. If
we transpose this passion to the level of the collective,
looking to what might be called for as part of our planetary initiation and the "good death" that it calls for, we
start to see how the need for reconciliation that Jem has
highlighted as essential to his proposed deep adaptation
agenda "invites reconciliation between peoples, genders,
classes, generations, countries, religions and political
persuasions. Because it is time to make our peace."[19]

Whatever reconciliation might be achieved at the
level of the collective will doubtless demand a great deal
of moral courage and, alongside the desire for peace, a

19. Bendell, "Hope and Vision."

passionate commitment to truth and justice. Though our histories already include long and unbroken traditions of struggle for liberation, we can perhaps see the mounting wave of holding actions and proposals for more Gaian structures—from the Black Lives Matter and Me Too movements to the many expressions of "Blockadia" (such as the iconic action at Standing Rock), the Extinction Rebellion and Sunrise movements, and calls for a Green New Deal—as evidence that a growing segment of the population is prepared not only to make peace, but to make things right. Some years ago now, Paul Hawken (2007) used the term "blessed unrest" to describe the "largest social movement in the world" that no one saw coming.[20] This movement for social justice and environmental integrity has only continued to grow and become more coherent in the intervening years. Not surprisingly, these same years have seen the breaking into the collective consciousness of the prospect of climate chaos and the Great Dying, which before most had not seen coming either (despite the early warnings). As more and more people start to lose whatever version of hope they have been affirming, will this blessed unrest give way to mere anarchy? Or will leaders of the movement draw new strength and inspiration to work for the good, because, as Jem puts it, "we have a faith or sense that this is the right way to be alive, not because it will work," and perhaps not even because we think there is still at least a chance that it could work? "The world we once knew is never coming back," writes climate scientist, Kate Marvel. "I have no hope that these changes can be reversed…. We need courage, not hope…." "Courage," she adds, "is the resolve to do well without the assurance of

---

20. P. Hawken, *Blessed Unrest: How the Largest Social Movement in History Is Restoring Grace, Justice, and Beauty to the World* (New York: Penguin Books, 2008).

a happy ending."[21] Commenting on the meteoric rise of the Extinction Rebellion movement and the philosophy underlying its remarkably effective activism as expressed in a catalyzing presentation by one of its founders, Roger Hallam, Dougald Hine notes that

> those whose willingness to act endures the longest are not the activists who are motivated by outcome, who need to be given hope and to believe in their chances of success, but the ones who are motivated by doing the right thing. It's the first time I can remember seeing a call to action which explicitly invites people to go into despair. In the closing minutes of his talk, Roger speaks about 'the dark night of the soul', the need to move through the darkness rather than avoid it. This is a call to rebellion that is framed in the language and draws on the traditions of mysticism.[22]

And there is still much that we can do well in whatever time we have left. Having passed willingly through the Gate of Hell, with hearts and minds open to the "suffering city"—honoring our pain for the world, as Joanna and others have encouraged us to do—we find new sources of courage and passion for justice. Along with planetary hospice work and the many struggles for liberation, for saving what we can of our lands and forests, our precious waters, and the dwindling numbers of our other-than-human siblings, I am inspired by the movement for climate justice and climate reparations, perhaps the most consequential expression of an integral

21. K. Marvel, "We Need Courage, Not Hope, To Face Climate Change," *On Being*, March 1, 2018, https://onbeing.org/blog/kate-marvel-we-need-courage-not-hope-to-face-climate-change/ (accessed May 3, 2020).
22. D. Hine, "After We Stop Pretending," *The Dark Mountain Project*, April 22, 2019, https://dark-mountain.net/after-we-stop-pretending/ (accessed May 3, 2020).

ecological approach to the planetary climate crisis. This movement acknowledges that the more affluent and first to industrialize nations are responsible for the majority of past carbon emissions and have benefited at the cost of so-called developing nations (through slavery, other forms of colonial domination, resource extraction, and "structural adjustment"). The latter have already and will continue to suffer most from the effects of climate chaos. Along with granting preferential assistance to disadvantaged nations in their attempt to implement standard forms of climate mitigation (reduction of emissions, transition to clean energy, energy efficiency, carbon capture, etc.) climate reparations should include radical reform of immigration policies to address the accelerating crisis of climate migrations.[23]

In my adoptive country of the United States of America, I would single out two pressing matters of unfinished business: genuine repentance for the genocide of this land's indigenous peoples and for the treatment of those who survived, and an honoring of promises made; repentance for the sin of slavery, acknowledging the critical

23. In "The Case for Climate Reparations," Olúfémi O. Táíwò and Beba Cibralic write: "Climate colonialism is like climate apartheid on an international scale. Economic power, location, and access to resources determine how communities can respond to climate impacts. But these factors are shaped by existing global injustices: the history of slavery, colonialism, and imperialism that enriched some countries at the expense of others. Global warming has exacerbated these inequalities, and the climate crisis will lead to new divisions between those who can mitigate its impact and those who cannot." "The great climate migration that will transform the world is just beginning. To adapt, the international community will need a different approach to politics. There are two ways forward: climate reparations or climate colonialism. Reparations would use international resources to address inequalities caused or exacerbated by the climate crisis; it would allow for a way out of the climate catastrophe by tackling both mitigation and migration. The climate colonialism alternative, on the other hand, would mean the survival of the wealthiest and devastation for the world's most vulnerable people." https://foreignpolicy.com/2020/10/10/case-for-climate-reparations-crisis-migration-refugees-inequality/ (accessed October 21, 2020).

role of African slaves and their descendants in building whatever greatness this country once enjoyed, and reparations to those now alive who still suffer from this sin.

And of course, in this country as elsewhere around the world, there is still much work to do around the dismantling of patriarchy and the kind of gender reconciliation that this would entail.

It is only by attending to this kind of unfinished business, by engaging in radical forms of truth and reconciliation, that we might transform our sojourn in Hell into something like Dante's ascent of Mount Purgatory. Here we can at least believe that the sin and suffering, the wrongs done, if they cannot be undone, can somehow be redeemed. For those who have already abandoned or relinquished hope, there is perhaps still a path of purification we can choose to follow, guided and sustained by a new kind of faith.

A Third Kind of Faith

In a recent interview,[24] Joanna imagines a reporter stopping Frodo as he journeys through the depths of Mordor on his quest to destroy the ring of power, asking him something like the following: "Are you hopeful or optimistic that you will make it to Mt. Doom?" Paraphrasing, Joanna has Frodo reply with a hand gesture similar to waving a pestering fly out one's face, and saying something like, "Get out of here! I don't have time for this!" In other words, in these end times, stopping to determine whether or not one has hope can be a distraction from the matter at hand. If we imagine Frodo as having relinquished hope, or at least having suspended the question of hope, it is clear that he has retained a

24. "Power of Community Online Summit: Climate Change and Consciousness," February 2019.

175

steadfast *faith*—faith in the absolute value of his mission and in the virtues this mission unconditionally affirms, in this case: fellowship, truthfulness, the essential goodness of creation, love.

I have already referred above to two kinds of faith. My thinking here is inspired by Edgar Morin's call for the cultivation of a new, third kind of religion. According to Edgar (who, along with Joanna, I have been blessed to count as friend and mentor), the first kind, which began to be eroded from the time of the Enlightenment, was a religion of salvation, of an otherworldly God or gods. The second kind of religion, typified in both Marxism and positivism or scientism (which latter is still the dominant worldview of much of the educated elite), did not recognize itself as a religion, though it still held up the promise of (this-worldly) salvation. The third kind of religion would be a "religion in the minimal sense suggested in one derivation of the word,"[25] at the heart of which would be the fact and ideal of planetary "re-liance" (also from the Latin: *re-ligare*: to fasten or join back together). The fact: the eco-social interdependence of all members of the Earth community. The ideal: this interdependence is something that needs to be recognized, affirmed, protected, and ever renewed. As I quoted in Chapter 1, the new religion of reliance, writes Edgar, would be

> a depth religion, uniting people in suffering and death.... Such a religion would lack any providence, any shining hereafter, but would bind us together as fellows in the unknown adventure.
>
> Such a religion would not have promises but roots: roots in our cultures and civilizations, in planetary and human history; roots in life; roots in the stars that have forged the atoms of which we are made; roots in the

25. Morin with Kern, *Homeland Earth*, 141.

cosmos where the particles were born and out of which our atoms were made. . . .

Such a religion would involve a belief, like all religions but, unlike other religions that repress doubt through excessive zeal, it would make room for doubt within itself. It would look out onto the abyss.[26]

This religion, though lacking the naïve confidence of earlier forms of faith, would possess what might be called meta-fidence, or metáfidence, the prefix "meta-" here suggesting both "after" and "beyond." Such metáfidence signals a radical position or disposition of the heart-mind, *after* the relinquishment of hope and of the two earlier forms of faith. It is still a kind of faith, however, in that it involves what the heart-mind believes and affirms as a highest good. As we saw in Chapter 4, Edgar captures the spirit of this good with the maxim: *"aimez pour vivre, vivez pour aimer!"*—*love for the sake of life, live for the sake of love!* As for love, Edgar notes that it concentrates in itself the power of "communion, enchantment, fervor, ecstasy; it lets us live the life of non-separation in separation, the life of the sacred, the adoration of a mortal, evanescent, and fragile being." He adds: "Love the fragile and perishable, for the best and most precious of things—including consciousness, beauty, and the soul—are fragile and perishable."[27]

The abyss that Edgar enjoins us to look out onto includes not only the fact of our existential finitude, the inevitability of suffering and death, but also the great Mystery of life itself, of the "unknown adventure" of cosmic evolution, which, in these end times, has achieved a level of self-consciousness on a planetary scale. In terms of Tolkien's epic tale, we could say that this abyss is not

26. Ibid., 142.
27. Morin, *La Méthode 6: Éthique*, 157, 232 (my translation).

only that of the Crack of Doom on the edge of which
Frodo and Gollum stand poised as the dark power of
Sauron threatens to engulf Middle Earth, but also the
great expanse of the western seas that stretch out from
the port of the Grey Havens, beyond whose waters lies
Valinor, also known as the Undying Lands. Though he
recognizes and celebrates the great Mystery, Edgar himself is either silent or even at times dismissive of the idea
of such a beyond in any literal sense. All of the major
world religions, of course, have their own versions of
this beyond, their various kinds of heaven, including a
highest or best heaven which is our true origin and destiny. While I too do not believe in the literal, materialistic
existence of such a heaven, I do hold to the truth of some
kind of spiritual "beyond" (the other sense of "meta"),
a beyond revealed or intuited as the depth dimension (or
dimensions) of reality or the cosmos itself, dimensions
which remain invisible to those confined to what Blake
calls "Single vision and Newton's sleep."[28]

To guard against self-deception and the temptation
of escapism, however, any talk of "beyond" in these end
times must be accompanied by an unshakeable resolution, like the Bodhisattva vow, to abide in the here and
now, as hellish as it might be or become. It is as though
the way to the Undying Lands runs through the center
of Gaia as a kind of Earth-sized Mandala. I am thinking
here of the practice known as the "Truth Mandala" in
Joanna's Work that Reconnects (itself a powerful expression of planetary re-liance). In this practice, participants
are convened around a sacred circle and invited, as

28. From a letter of William Blake to Thomas Butt (November 22, 1802): "Now
I a fourfold vision see/And a fourfold vision is given to me/Tis fourfold in my supreme delight/And three fold in soft Beulahs night/And twofold Always. May God
us keep/From Single vision & Newtons sleep." *The Letters of William Blake with
Related Documents*. 3rd ed. Ed. G. Keynes, Kt (Oxford: Clarendon Press, 1980), 46.

the spirit moves them, to enter into one or more of the quadrants where, assisted by a ritual object (dry leaves for grief, a stone for fear, a stick for anger, and an empty bowl for the sense of deprivation and powerlessness) they can speak, and honor, their pain for the world. This ritual is not merely cathartic, since what emerges in the end is the insight that this pain is an expression of a deeper solidarity with the greater Life in which we are embedded. Our anger, Joanna reminds us, is rooted in our passion for justice. It takes enormous courage to be honest about our fear. The deprivation and powerlessness we feel is a signal of our interdependence, and we only grieve what we love and that to which, despite the loss, we still feel bound, still affirm and embrace.

The Fullness of Time

In the Spiral of the Work that Reconnects, the station of honoring our pain for the world allows for, and is followed by, that of "seeing with new eyes." Here the teachings and practices are designed to facilitate an experience of our deeper identities, beyond the "skin-encapsulated ego," as living members of Gaia, the living and sacred Earth. These teachings and practices draw from systems theory, the deep history of the journey of the universe, and the world's many wisdom traditions. A particular focus in this part of the work has to do with our changing sense of time. Most people are not aware that the human experience of time has evolved over the millennia. For countless ages all the way to the early modern period, humans experienced time in terms of the regular and endlessly repeating cycles of nature, of birth and death, of the seasons and stars. That began to change, slowly at first with the spread of the first mechanical clocks, then more quickly and pervasively once the industrial revolution eventually, and quite recently, gave rise to a new

Figure 2: The Great Acceleration (note the inflection point around 1950)

geological sphere superimposed on the biosphere—the technologically mediated anthroposphere—along with its new geological age, the Anthropocene. Though some see the first signs of the Anthropocene as far back as the agricultural revolution, I agree with those who see it as coinciding with the Great Acceleration beginning around 1950 (see figure 2.).

It is difficult to say whether it is along with, or because of, all of these accelerating socio-economic and Earth system trends that our sense of the passage of time has been accelerating as well. The exponential character of these trends (and indeed, faster than exponential for some of them) is best captured by the following two graphs (atmospheric CO_2 and rate of species extinction), which are also perhaps the two most consequential as indicators of these end times.

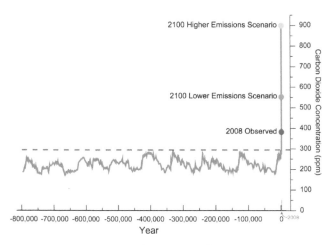

Figure 3: CO_2 over time (note that the timeline has been moved up since this 2008 assessment from 2100 to 2050)

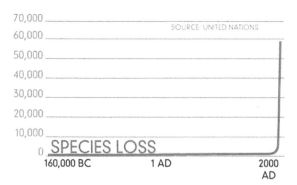

Figure 4: rate of extinction

Many of us are painfully familiar with the distressing feelings of compression and anxiety accompanying this acceleration, particularly, of course, when the apocalyptic potential of these two graphs is taken to heart. It is as though we are being pressed up against a wall, with no possibility of escape. Or if we were to lay these graphs on their sides, the wall would become the edge of the abyss and the threshold of initiation on which we are poised, promising its own planetary NDE.

Some see the Great Acceleration as pointing toward the inevitable convergence of certain trends (renewable energy, artificial intelligence, bio- and nanotechnology, 3D printing) toward a technological Singularity which could, in principle, pull us away from the abyss. Personally, I don't see how such a Singularity, even if it did arrive within the next few decades, could manifest its potential benefits fast enough to counter the unravelling of the web of life and the collapse of the civilizational infrastructure upon which advanced technologies, along with we humans, would continue to depend. Peter Russell, one of the first people to speculate on the broader implications of a technological Singularity and its associated accelerating trends, now believes in the inevitability of overreach and collapse. He leaves open the possibility of some kind of technological Singularity that might precede collapse. Peter stresses the non-linear and exponential character of the rate of acceleration in which we are being swept up. Not only the rate of change, but the rate of acceleration is itself accelerating. Once again we are presented with a kind of wall, or "blind spot," as Peter calls it, beyond which we cannot peer.

As for whatever time we have left, "Our species may be gone in a century or so," he writes,

> but that does not mean it is all for nothing. Quite the opposite. We may have little future in terms of linear

time, but in exponential time so much more is possible. In the coming decades there may be as much development as has happened in the whole of human history. Or perhaps even more. Within the short linear time remaining for our species we may yet come to a complete knowing of the world, both around us and within us. This does not mean knowing everything it is possible to know, but everything this particular intelligence could know in this biological form, from this point in the universe.[29]

Certainly, in terms of our knowledge of natural systems, though one can expect and even celebrate an unresolved Mystery at the base, we already possess a coherent account of the nature, evolution, and probable destiny of the cosmos. The details are inexhaustible, but the grand lines of the whole have been revealed. As we saw in Chapter 3, this includes all the major thresholds of evolution, from the Big Bang or "primal Flaring Forth" (as Thomas Berry and Brian Swimme call it) some 13.6 billion years ago and the birth of particles, light, and galaxies shortly after, through the ignition of stars, the formation of Earth, and the birth of life, to the late emergence of our species some 200 to 300,000 years ago, the last moments of whose history have brought the planet to this new threshold. Berry writes: "While perhaps incomplete, the narrative as given here presents in outline the story of the universe and of the planet Earth as this story is now available to us. This is our sacred story. It is our way of dealing with the mystery whence all things come into being."[30]

29. P. Russell, "Blind Spot: The Unforeseen End of Accelerating Change," 16, https://www.peterrussell.com/blindspot/blindspot.pdf (accessed May 3, 2020).
30. Berry, *The Sacred Universe*, 110.

Lifting the Veil

A great paradox of these end times, and a great gift, is that the looming apocalypse not only threatens death and destruction, but offers a more general access to certain kinds of knowledge and experience that, until now, had been reserved for a few saints, shamans, mystics, or specialists in philosophy and religion. For many, and already for some time now, the Wall has become a transparent veil, and the veil itself has been lifted, however momentarily. This is, after all, the literal meaning of *apokalyptein*: "to uncover or reveal." The new story of the universe is clearly an integral part of this revelation. In terms of the human part of this journey, though so much has been lost, it is also the case that never before has so much of the diverse cultural productions of humanity—languages, myths, symbols, literature, histories, cosmologies, philosophies, religious teachings and practices, whether indigenous, Asian, or Western—been widely available, immediately and without a fee or the need for formal initiation. Of course, such access does not necessarily translate into genuine understanding or wisdom. Still, an effect of the virtualization of planetary cultural history and its stores of knowledge is to make all times past, and places, in some sense present.

Whether or not the technological Singularity ever comes to pass, we could say that the exponential acceleration of human actions and interactions has already reached such a pitch that the fabric of linear time has stretched in places to the point of becoming transparent, if not of tearing altogether. This transparency or *diaphaneity*, as Jean Gebser also calls it, is a defining feature of the "aperspectival" or *integral* age whose dawn he announced at the onset of the Great Acceleration in his dense but brilliant book, *The Ever-Present Origin* (1949–1953). Origin (*Ursprung* in German) is another word for the Mystery whose nature, according to Gebser, has revealed itself through a series of mutations of consciousness with their own distinctive experience of both space and time. The modern mutation into perspectival (mental)[31] consciousness, with its linear time and purely quantitative space (epitomized by the mechanistic worldviews of Descartes and Newton), was preceded by the pre-perspectival (magical and mythic) experience of cyclical time and qualitative space. The dawning integral age is also the mutation into *a*perspectival consciousness (one might also say *meta*-perspectival). The diaphaneity of the integral-aperspectival allows for the co-presence or appropriate alternation between the magical, mythic, and mental structures of consciousness along with their specific experiences of space and time.

With respect to time, the integral-aperspectival structure allows for a "consciousness of the whole," a consciousness "encompassing all time and embracing both …[the] distant past and…approaching future as a living present." This present, he tells us, is "the undivided presence of yesterday, today, and tomorrow" which "in a consciously realized actualization can…encompass origin as an ineradicable present."[32] This is very close to Zen master Dogen's notion of *uji*, or "time-being" (usually translated to match the order of the Japanese characters as "being-time"), which he derived from direct insight into the core Buddhist teaching of the dependent co-arising of all phenomena (*pratītyasamutpāda*). Dogen writes: "Each moment is all being, is the entire world. Reflect now whether any being or any world is left out of the present moment."

31. Gebser's use of "perspectival" does not refer to the postmodern idea of perspectivism or constructivism, but to the new way of seeing the world signaled by the development of linear perspective in art and design.

32. Gebser, *The Ever-Present Origin*, 6, 294.

Do not think that time merely flies away. Do not see flying away as the only function of time. If time merely flies away, you would be separated from time. The reason you do not clearly understand the time-being is that you think of time as only passing.

In essence, all things in the entire world are linked with one another as moments. Because all moments are the time-being, they are your time-being.[33]

Gebser, for his part, offers an enormous amount of evidence for his claims, drawing from the natural and social sciences, from philosophy and religious studies, the history of science and of the arts, and more. Nevertheless, unless one has had some taste of the kinds of consciousness of which he speaks, his account might seem abstract and obscure. This is especially the case when he explains what he means by Origin or the integral. Gebser is compelled to invent new words and phrases for the occasion, as with the words *diaphanon*, *aperspectival*, or the *achronon*, which latter he also renders as "time-freedom", echoing Dogen's "time-being". The experience of Origin or the integral brings with it a freedom from linear clock time (*chronos*) and the crushing pressure of relentless acceleration. Though Gebser brings considerable mental effort in trying to characterize the nature of Origin and the growing diaphaneity of the integral age, he leaves no doubt that the mental structure, with its neat conceptual distinctions, is alone insufficient to the task. Some kind of direct experience is essential.

If Gebser makes for challenging reading, Dogen's path of zazen is likely too narrow to accommodate the many who, in these end times, feel pressed up against the wall of the Great Acceleration. Though we will continue

33. Dogen, *Moon In a Dewdrop: Writings of Zen Master Dogen* (New York: North Point Press, 1995), 77-78.

to be nourished by the lives and teachings of the great masters of awakening, we need new ways as well, such as Stan Grof's holotropic therapy, other forms of consciousness exploration, and the practices that Joanna has developed in the Work that Reconnects that allow those with sufficient moral imagination to enter into what she calls the "fourth time" (a term she borrows from Tibetan Buddhism), a time within which we can reclaim our solidarity with all of our ancestors—human, other-than-human, and cosmic—as well as with the future beings, all of whom "surround us like a cloud of witnesses."[34] In the practice called "Harvesting the gifts of the ancestors," for example, one is guided into an embodied identification with the lives of countless generations who have walked before us, honoring their struggles and drawing strength from their virtues. In the practice of "The Seventh Generation," we find ourselves sitting face to face with a future being, or we ourselves temporarily embody this future being, from whose perspective we are graced with new and vivid insights pertaining to our present time of the Great Unraveling and Great Turning.

Blossoms

In the first years co-teaching with Joanna, it was still possible for me to imagine that, seven generations from now, we will have beaten the odds and succeeded in making the transition to a life-sustaining civilization. The last time we offered the course together on the Great Turning at the California Institute of Integral Studies, and in the times I have facilitated the work since then, the odds have shifted dramatically. Some of the future beings, at least, have delivered messages from a post-apocalyptic world. Though still speaking to us with gratitude and

34. Macy and Johnstone, *Active Hope*, 160.

compassion for our roles in these end times, some of these new voices no longer sing songs of the success of the Great Turning, or they are inviting us to rethink the nature of the Great Turning in ways that might allow us to keep walking while heeding the inscription over the Gate.

If indeed it transpires that the future we have to look forward to is relatively brief and increasingly grim, what kind of consolation, it might be asked, does the kind of integral vision and its experience of the fourth time explored above hold for us in these end times? Is it enough, as Peter Russell invites us to do, to

> celebrate all that we have become, while accepting that we are here only for a brief flash of cosmic time? A friend reminds me of the so-called century plant that flowers once in 20 or so years. When it does finally bloom, we marvel at the ten-foot long stalk, holding high a magnificent array of yellow-flowered branches. The spectacle is made all the more awesome by the knowing that it flowers but once; then dies, its purpose complete. Can we celebrate ourselves in a similar light? Another blossoming in the cosmos. An exquisitely beautiful flowering of consciousness. A miracle of creation.[35]

Of course, we could ask the same question with regard to our individual lives, each of which, however long, will eventually be rounded into a relative moment. This is even more the case for a long life, since as we age, the days, weeks, and months perform their own version of the Great Acceleration. For some, the poignancy of life's impermanence is consolation enough, especially if one retains the sense of an inscrutable Mystery behind it all. We see this attitude in Edgar's version of a third kind

---

35. Russell, "Blind Spot," 19.

of religion, and perhaps in its most developed form in the classical Japanese appreciation for *mono no aware* (usually translated as "the pathos of things"). Human civilization, the blossom of a century plant, and our individual lives, so many cherry blossom petals carried on the wind.

For many, however, such an attitude is not enough. Can we glean more from a third kind of faith? Here I can only offer my own reflections, which may or may not resonate with your own intuition and experiences. For my part, I have to come to terms—repeatedly, it would seem—with the loss of so many I have known and loved—starting with the sudden death of my father when I was seven, and over the years, my grandparents and mother, a sister, over two-dozen aunts and uncles, and several very close friends. And there are all the sweet places, encounters, achievements, countless precious moments, all so many petals in the wind. If I then set this life within the fading blossom of human civilization and possibly of complex life itself, I for one require something beyond naked existential affirmation or aesthetic ecstasy, even if accompanied by an otherwise mute sense of the Mystery. To what, then, might I turn for consolation?

Consolations of Philosophy

Boethius wrote his *Consolation of Philosophy* some 1500 years ago during the slow collapse of the Roman empire, imprisoned while awaiting execution for trumped up charges of treason. As we face our own prospect of collapse and collective death, some of us can still be inspired and consoled by the instruction Boethius received from "Lady Philosophy." Following discussions on the nature of true happiness, evil, free will, and providence, the work culminates with a meditation on time and eternity. We are told that what to us, as finite beings,

189

is experienced as a continuous sequence of events in linear time, with the past exerting its causal influence on the
present and the present determining the conditions for
the future, for God or the infinite Divine mind is always
and already grasped as eternally present. "His knowledge," the Lady tells us, "...passes over every change of
time, embracing infinite lengths of past and future, views
in its own direct comprehension everything as though it
were taking place in the present."[36] I have no doubt that,
though expressed in philosophical (and gender-inflected)
terms along with many telling analogies, this teaching arose out of his intuition or experience of integral
time,[37] necessarily couched, however, in the language and
worldview of his age. The same would seem to be true of
Dante some eight hundred years later, judging from the
poetic rendering of his mystical vision at the end of his
journey through Paradise. Gazing into the radiant center
of the Rose Mandala of the Godhead, he writes:

> Within its depths I saw gathered together,
> Bound by love into a single volume,
> Leaves that lie scattered through the universe.
> Substance and accidents and their relations
> I saw as though they fused in such a way
> That what I say is but a gleam of light.[38]
> ...
> Because the Good, the object of the will,
> Is gathered all in it, and out of it

36. Boethius, *The Consolation of Philosophy*, trans. W.V. Cooper (Grand Rapids: J. M. Dent, 1902), 71.

37. For my extended proposal for the notion of integral time, see S. Kelly, "Integral Time and the Varieties of Post-Mortem Survival," *Integral Review* 4.1 (2008): 5-30. http://integral-review.org/integral-time-and-the-varieties-of-post-mortem-survival/ (accessed May 3, 2020).

38. Dante, *Paradiso*, Canto 33, lines 85–90. Dante, *The Divine Comedy, Revised Edition*, Trans. James Finn Cotter (Forum Italicum: 2000).

Figure 5: The White
Rose of Paradise

The thing that there is perfect has some flaw.
Now shall my telling of what I remember
Fall far below the babbling of a baby
Still bathing its tongue at the mother's breast.
Not that there is more than a single semblance
Within that living Light on which I looked
And which is always what it was before,
But by the sight that gathered strength in me
As I gazed on, what was One in appearance
Was altering for me as I was changing.[39]

I could cite many other instances, from both Christian and non-Christian sources, of this intuition or experience of what scholars of mysticism refer to as the eternal present (*nunc stans*). By all accounts, it can be a deep and blessed consolation to those graced with such an

39. Ibid., lines 104–14.

experience, as it has been in my own case. It is important to note, however, that the eternal present evoked by Boethius and Dante is still in tension with the realm of finitude and its division into the three times. Boethius is ever reminding us of the vanity of this world and imploring us to direct our gaze heavenward. Dante's Heaven, similarly, is pictured as existing completely outside the cosmos, with Hell in fact being situated at its very center in the bowels of Earth. At the same time, however, Dante's world picture is contradicted by the beatific vision with which the *Comedia* culminates, where "Within its depths I saw gathered together, Bound by love into a single volume, Leaves that lie scattered through the universe." This tension is typical of the dominant strains of all the major world religions and philosophies which arose during the first Axial Age (c. 8th to 3rd centuries BCE). As we saw in Chapter 1, the mutation of consciousness from the mythic to the mental structure that occurred at that time seems to have required this tension to stabilize its newly grasped ideal of conceptual and ethical universality. This ideal of universality presented a momentous achievement in the evolution of consciousness and provided a precious consolation to those seeking release from a world of impermanence, suffering, and death. Though the details are too numerous and complex to present here,[40] I and others have come to understand how this mutation also eventually made possible the rise of modern science (with its quest for universal natural laws) and technology which, as they grew in power, became the basis for a second kind of religion, or at least a substitute religion, with its promises of earthly rather than heavenly salvation. As we know, though the sciences themselves have indeed provided the basis for a genuine revelation in the form of the

40. See Kelly, *Coming Home.*

new story of the universe, and despite the many comforts and improvements afforded by modern industrial technology, the second kind of religion's promises of endless progress into a radiant future increasingly ring false as more of us waken to these end times.

Still, it would be a mistake to lose sight of the deeper intention that seems to be at work in the wider arc of the evolution of consciousness, an intention discernible in the non-dual intuitions already present in the esoteric core of the great Axial traditions. For these end times are also times of planetary awakening. The death sentence that we are being called to face, the Hell and Purgatory that we must walk through, are themselves somehow integral to a new kind of "Heaven"—not on, but somehow *of*, Earth—with its own, more concrete embodiment of universality proper to a third kind religion or faith.

Confessions

As a child, I was nourished by the rituals and symbols of Roman Catholicism, which I took in naively but with a genuine sense of their numinous power. Like many of my peers, I lost this first naïve faith (though not my appreciation for the core symbols) shortly after puberty, at which point, for a brief time, I could worship at the altar of modern science and technology (the second kind of faith). A path that might have led to a career in the scientific priesthood was diverted by my initiation during my teens into the mysteries of psychedelic experience. I eventually also became more conscious of the shadow of scientific progress, wedded as it has been to the devastations of industrial growth society. Baptized anew in the last waves of the 60s Counterculture, but prompted as well by my native disposition, I chose to study the humanities, though I retained my deep appreciation for the natural sciences as well.

Aside from the formative psychedelic experiences of my teens, I have been visited from early childhood and periodically throughout my life with spontaneous "peak experiences," and in particular with moments of what James calls "noetic certainty" that, somehow, though everything undeniably passes, nothing is lost. These moments of intuitive certainty regarding the nature of integral time have been confirmed and filled out during my adult life in the context of ritually structured sacred medicine journeys, a sporadic sitting practice (to begin with in the Theravadin tradition, then Tibetan, then Zen), my regular practice of *zhan zhuang* (a form of standing meditation developed within the Chinese internal martial arts), and my forty some years of research as a contemplative scholar of philosophy, religion, and the evolution of consciousness. These years have deepened and shaped my own understanding and practice of a third kind of faith.

Along with the inspiration I have received from Edgar, Joanna, and Gebser, my own practice of this faith has been nourished by the insights of the 20th century Hindu sage, Sri Aurobindo, from whom Gebser borrowed the term "integral" to describe the mutation of consciousness now upon us. Clearly tapping into the same kind of insight we saw in Boethius, Dogen, and Dante, though without the negative valuation of time and finitude typical of the dominant expressions of the great first Axial traditions, we find this remarkable passage from the last chapter of his book, *The Synthesis of Yoga*, devoted to "the supramental time vision." "All intuitive knowledge," writes Aurobindo,

> comes more or less directly from the light of the self-aware spirit entering into the mind, the spirit concealed behind mind and conscious of all in itself and in all its selves, omniscient and capable of illumining the ignorant or the self-forgetful mind whether by rare or

constant flashes or by a steady instreaming light, out of its omniscience. This all includes all that was, is or will be in time and this omniscience is not limited, impeded or baffled by our mental division of the three times and the idea and experience of a dead and no longer existent and ill-remembered or forgotten past and a not yet existent and therefore unknowable future which is so imperative for the mind in the ignorance. Accordingly the growth of the intuitive mind can bring with it the capacity of a time knowledge which comes to it not from outside indices, but from within the universal soul of things, its eternal memory of the past, its unlimited holding of things present and its prevision or, as it has been paradoxically but suggestively called, its memory of the future.[41]

Again, it might be impossible for those with no acquaintance at all with this kind of intuition to relate to what Aurobindo is saying here about the "the universal soul of things," a self-aware spirit "behind" but also inclusive of our normal mental awareness. If, however, as I believe and can confirm from my own experience (though clearly in no way at the level of an Aurobindo), these words speak true, what are the implications for how we can understand and navigate these end times?

The Other God of the Philosophers[42]

The first kind of faith (in otherworldly salvation) which has been continually eroded since the birth of modernity has always been accompanied by a less well-

41. Aurobindo, *Synthesis of Yoga* (Pondicherry: Sri Aurobindo Ashram Press, 1999), 896.
42. I take this phrase from the title of the book by J.W. Cooper, *Panentheism: The Other God of the Philosophers: From Plato to the Present* (Grand Rapids: Baker Academic, 2006).

known philosophical and theological sibling technically known as *panentheism*. The classical theism of the first kind of faith is committed to a belief in God or the divine (as infinite and eternal) existing completely outside the cosmos (the finite realm of space and time). Panentheists, by contrast, understand the all (*pan*) or cosmos as existing within (*en*) God or the divine (*theos*), which also exists *in* everything. The panentheist tradition is richly varied and has found a home in all world religions. It is this tradition, I believe, which has most to offer those who are open to more fully developed expressions of a third kind of faith. Aside from the fact that, from a philosophical point of view, it is arguably the only coherent form of religion or spirituality committed to the ideal of universality, panentheism also has significant pragmatic advantages when considering the psychospiritual demands of living in end times.[43]

As an experiment, examine the feeling-tone that accompanies you imagining your life, from as long as you can remember to this moment right now, as a mere sequence of events without foundation, intrinsic value, or lasting importance—in other words, as Macbeth's tale told by an idiot, signifying nothing. Now imagine and feel into the image of this same life, and indeed the entire history of the cosmos, as unfolding within the living and luminous body of the Divine. I realize that many people will consider the latter a mere metaphysical fantasy. I would not try to convince them otherwise (even if I may have done so in the past) especially if they are content with their role in the other tale. For those who resonate

---

43. For a discussion of some philosophical, religious, and scientific dimensions of panentheism, see S. Kelly, "Evolutionary Panentheism for the Planetary Era: A Gallery of Images," Seven Pillars House of Wisdom, November 10, 2009, http://www.sevenpillarshouse.org/article/evolutionary_panentheism_for_the_planetary_era/ (accessed May 3, 2020).

with my own experience, however—or at least for those willing to exercise their moral imagination—I invite you at least to consider the implications of such a panentheistic vision. Along with the consolation of feeling embraced within the cosmos as the living body of God (rather than merely being afloat in the infinite expanse of a mechanistic universe), there is the potential of awakening to its own higher-dimensional, integral time, where your life and all others, as Blake puts it, rest "Permanent and not lost, not lost nor vanish'd, and every little act, Word, work, and wish that has existed, all remaining still ... One hair nor particle of dust not one can pass away."[44] We find an exquisite evocation of this other God of the philosophers in Rilke's poem, "The Buddha in glory" (which, though I doubt that Rilke was aware of it, seems to be addressed to Mahavairocana, the cosmic Buddha of esoteric Buddhism):

> Center of all centers, core of cores,
> almond self-enclosed and growing sweet–
> all this universe, to the furthest stars
> and beyond them, is your flesh, your fruit.
>
> Now you feel how nothing clings to you;
> your vast shell reaches into endless space,
> and there the rich, thick fluids rise and flow.
> Illuminated in your infinite peace,
>
> a billion stars go spinning through the night,
> blazing high above your head.
> But in you is the presence that
> will be, when all the stars are dead.[45]

44. William Blake, "Jerusalem: The Emanation of the Giant Albion," plates 13 & 14.

45. R.M. Rilke, "Buddha in Glory," in *Ahead of All Parting: The Selected Poetry and Prose of Rainer Maria Rilke*, trans. Stephen Mitchell (New York: Modern Library, 1995), 75.

From the mental perspective of linear time, countless stars have already died, as our sun too will die (it is currently about half-way through its ten-billion year life cycle), along with Earth and the rest of the solar system. Long before then, of course, you and I and everyone we know will have passed, and the world as humans have always known it is passing as I write these lines. From the meta- or aperspective of integral time, however, all lives—of sun and Earth and you and I—each of their moments, *including the moments of passing*, abide as so many ever-living petals in the Rose Mandala of the true Heaven. For the true infinity of this Heaven, as Hegel reminds us, must include the finite (otherwise it would, through this exclusion, itself be rendered finite).

Whether through disciplined contemplation, peak experiences, or exercising the moral imagination, it is by awakening to our participation in this Mandala that we can draw strength from the ancestors who surround us "like a cloud of witnesses," those who, in their own times, have faced so many hardships, have been the vehicle for countless forms of creativity, have known victory over evil, and the resonant tones of whose lives even now ring out like a mantra of blessing. And not only our human ancestors, but all of our cosmic and Gaian kin, the fruits of whose evolutionary adventures we rehearsed in our mother's womb and are enfolded in each of our cells. As for the future ones, however many generations there will be, from the meta-perspective of integral time we are already their ancestors. Regardless of how many or few will at some point remain, surely they will need to draw on the strength and courage we are being called upon to manifest in our own time.

A Light in the Darkness

And if our future as a species is short, if the abyss we are hurtling towards promises not only a collective *near-death* experience, but a transition through the Great Dying already upon us to the Great Silence that would seem to follow? We are brought back to our earlier consideration of a terminal diagnosis and unfinished business. From the meta-perspective of integral time, one could say that the length of time remaining is not so critical since, because nothing is really lost, each moment possesses its own intrinsic, and in some sense infinite, value. By the same token, however, the infinite character of integral time includes not only all moments, but their passing as well. The true infinite, as we have seen, must include the finite, which means that the passing, the dying too and everything that surrounds it, is embraced within the eternally living present of the greater Life in and through whom we have our being. In this way we can begin to intuit the infinite value or eternal significance of our actions in these end times—the love declared, the wrongs confessed or forgiven, the struggles entered into on the side of the true, the good, and the beautiful.[46] That these actions might be our last—and of course the same holds true for our individual lives—makes them all the more precious. To more easily grasp why this is so, I suggest the following negative analogies and invite you to pay particular attention to the accompanying feeling-tone. Imagine receiving a letter from your beloved that has taken weeks to reach you from a distant land, but somehow missing the last paragraph with its intimate goodbyes; or attending a performance of Beethoven's Ninth Symphony

46. I am convinced that the "greatest weight" that Nietzsche associated with his intuition of Eternal Recurrence arose from his own intuition of integral time (see my "Integral Time" above).

without the final few bars; or reading Keats's immortal ode without the closing lines: "Beauty is truth, truth beauty,—that is all/Ye know on earth, and all ye need to know."[47] Now imagine these without anything missing, their power and beauty made whole by a finishing touch.

If indeed nothing is lost, with "every little act, Word, work, and wish that has existed, all remaining still," this must include as well not only the passing of all moments, but all the missed opportunities, the experiences of failure, pain, of evil and suffering of all kinds. In this sense one might grant a qualified truth to the idea of an eternal Hell. This Hell, however, unlike the way it is pictured in Dante's poem and the popular imagination as the fallen center of Earth which stands opposite to and outside of God in Heaven, must rather be embraced by the panentheistic, integral infinite of the true Heaven, and redeemed in this embrace. Only from the dualistic point of view of the self-enclosed ego (however illusory this self-enclosure may be) are evil and suffering experienced as existing outside the Godhead. Recall the culmination of Dante's beatific vision where, gazing into the radiance of the Rose Mandala, we read: "In its profundity I saw— ingathered and bound by love into one single volume— what, in the universe, seems separate, scattered."

It is in this sense that I read the lines from the most mystical of the four gospels: "And the light shines in the darkness, and the darkness did not comprehend it" (*John* 1:5). The light "shines" (present tense, indicating the eternally living present of the true infinite) while the darkness (evil and suffering) "did not comprehend it" (past tense, indicating the exclusionary character of egoic consciousness and its linear time sense). "Comprehend" (κατέλαβεν) also has the meaning of "overcome" which

47. Keats, "Ode on a Grecian Urn."

suggests that, from the (meta)point of view of Absolute Spirit or the Whole, and despite localized appearances to the contrary, there is nowhere that the divine radiance does not in fact penetrate. In a manner remarkably analogous to the omnicentric view of contemporary Big Bang cosmology—where the "primal flaring forth" at the point of origin is said to coincide with every point in the expanding universe—we are led to the panentheistic intuition of the Godhead as, in Nicolas of Cusa's phrasing, an "infinite circle whose center is everywhere and whose circumference is nowhere."[48] I realize we are dealing with the deepest of mysteries here and, like Dante, my commentary undoubtedly falls "far below the babbling of a baby/Still bathing its tongue at the mother's breast."[49]

And the greatest of these...

Babbling though it may be, we should be grateful to have our tongues bathed at the mother's breast. By mother here I mean the "Queen of Heaven" who took pity on Dante and sent him both Virgil and Beatrice to guide him, the "Mother of God" who sits enthroned in the Rose Mandala of the true Heaven. To the Egyptians she was known as Isis "of Ten Thousand names". To the people of the Andes, She is Pachamama (the "World Mother"). She is Sophia, the Divine Wisdom, *Prajna-paramita* ("the perfection of wisdom"), the Mother of all Buddhas and Bodhisattvas, and the *Mahadevi* of Hinduism. As with the other God of the philosophers, this Mother is She in and through whom we have our

---

48. Nicholas of Cusa, *On Learned Ignorance*, in *Nicholas of Cusa: Selected Spiritual Writings*, H. Lawrence Bond, tr. (New York: Paulist Press, 1997), 61. Nicholas did not invent this formulation. Its earliest known source is the 12th Century *Book of the 24 Philosophers*. For the parallels with contemporary cosmology, see Kelly, *Coming Home*, 136.

49. Dante, *Paradiso*, Canto 31, lines 107–8.

Figure 6 (left): Prajnaparamita, the Mother of all Buddhas. Figure 7 (right): Vierge Ouvrante ("Opening Virgin)

being, the (intimate) All in which everything subsists and which pervades all that is, was, and shall be. As the Greek-Egyptian poet Isidorus sang to Isis more than two millennia ago: "Because of You heaven and the whole earth have their being."[50] This panentheistic vision of the Mother is beautifully captured in the medieval Christian *"Vierge Ouvrante"* ('opening Virgin") statues. Closed, the Virgin is seen holding the baby Jesus on her lap, in the inherited position of Isis with the infant Horus. When opened, Mary's womb is seen to contain the whole drama of incarnation and redemption, indeed even the triune Godhead of Father, Son, and Holy Spirit.

By all accounts it makes a world of difference—a whole cosmos, perhaps—if one has a conscious, heart-centered relationship to this Mother. In the absence of such, one can perhaps at least relate to the qualities

50. Isidorus, Hymn I of the four Greek Hymns to Isis.

or virtues She is said to embody and graciously transmit. The three that I would single out are faith, wisdom, and love. We have already considered the nature of a third kind of faith suited to these end times, one that, in the absence of hope, nevertheless "loves for the sake of life, and lives for sake of love." The life loved is the greater Life of the grand evolutionary adventure of which our precious Earth and each of its members—land and seas, animals and trees, the stars and clouds and seasons, you and me— are all integral expressions. The act of faith—for it is an act—involves an unconditional affirmation of this greater Life and its myriad expressions. This faith is an act of will issuing from the deepest center of the heart-mind and takes the form of a blessing, affirming in the words of the Creator in Genesis, though in the integral tense of the ever-living present: "It is good." And if we affirm but a single moment, as Nietzsche saw so clearly, and in a powerful evocation of the truth of dependent co-arising,

> we thus affirm not only ourselves but all existence. For nothing is self-sufficient, neither in us ourselves nor in things; and if our soul has trembled with happiness and sounded like a harp string just once, all eternity was needed to produce this one event—and in this single moment of affirmation all eternity was called good, redeemed, justified, and affirmed.[51]

As Nietzsche realized, however, such an ecstatic affirmation should in no way lead to a passive acceptance of the status quo, to the facile conclusion that "Whatever is, is right."[52] Though it may bless the Whole as good, the intuition of integral time carries with it the ethical im-

---

51. F. Nietzsche, *The Will to Power*, trans. W. Kaufmann and R. J. Hollingdale (New York: Random House, 1967), 532–33.
52. A. Pope, from *An Essay on Man*.

perative to *make* things good and right, regardless of the odds or prospects of success. It is this intuition, I believe, that is the secret source of Havel's conviction that we are moved to act because "something makes sense, regardless of how it turns out."

As for Wisdom, we are fortunate to have such a rich array of traditions to draw from, and so many sages to guide us.[53] Despite my high regard for Lao Ze's wise admonition that "Those who know, do not speak./ Those who speak, do not know," my own sense of the Wisdom that might guide us in these end times should be apparent from the many words I have already shared in these pages. It is a Wisdom of wholeness that embraces brokenness, of the infinite that overarches the finite, of eternity which, as Blake puts it, "is in love with the productions of time."[54] It is a Wisdom grounded in the intuition of the Whole or the Absolute as *complexio oppositorum* (Cusa, Jung), as the "identity of identity and non-identity" (Hegel), the "union of union and disunion" (Morin), as "multeity in unity" (Coleridge), the cosmic Logos made flesh, "the realization of Buddhahood by grasses

---

53. For myself, along with such remarkable twentieth century and contemporary figures as Aurobindo, Gebser, Jung, Edgar Morin, and Joanna Macy, I am nourished by several lines of what could be called integral non-dual wisdom teachings. Chief among them are the incarnational mystical tradition of Christianity, rooted in certain passages of the scriptures and taken up by so many over the past two millennia, including Meister Eckhart, Nicolas of Cusa, William Blake, Hegel, Teilhard de Chardin, Rudolf Steiner, Owen Barfield, Jung, and many others; and the Mahayana Buddhist scriptures and commentaries, beginning with the teachings of Prajnaparamita and stretching through the esoteric or Vajrayana teachings of Tibet, China, and Japan. Alongside these figures and traditions, I am inspired by the word's many indigenous wisdom traditions, both through texts, verbal transmission, and as I have experienced some of them directly in connection with encounters with plant medicines. Finally, I would have to include the profound and lasting impressions that the enchanted visions of Tolkien and other literary masters (including William Blake, John Cowper Powys, and too many poets to mention here) have had on the development of my moral imagination.

54. W. Blake, from *The Marriage of Heaven and Hell*.

and trees" (*somoku jobutsu*), and the insight that "Form does not differ from Emptiness/And Emptiness does not differ from Form" (*Heart Sutra*).

It should therefore be clear that, just as the third kind of faith includes doubt and uncertainty, so Wisdom must include the recognition of ineradicable ignorance. "Contemporary reflection," as Edgar reminds us, "must begin with the consciousness of the limits of knowledge, not so as to enclose itself within these limits, but in order to become a sentinel of the unknown and a satellite of the inconceivable."[55] It is a question, as Cusa saw so well half a millennium ago now, of a learnèd ignorance, of including the unknown within our knowing. This wise ignorance is not only learnèd —informed as it is by the kinds of insights we have engaged with throughout these pages—but must be learned. It is a coming to know that, and when, we don't know, yet also a growing knowl-edge-as-intimacy with the unknown, an encountering of that which escapes the grasp of the certainty-seeking ego. Paradoxically, the cultivation of such a wise ignorance does not diminish but rather invites the kind of courage needed to face the looming planetary abyss.

The letting go of the need for certainty—even as we might affirm more integral intuitions as an act of faith, and act with purpose and passion on the basis of this faith—is the counterpart of unconditional love, a love that both calls to us and is most called for in these end times. As we have seen, it is love for the sake of the greater Life, and we live this Life for the sake of love. Faith, Wisdom, and Love: a holy trinity for these end times, and for all times, but now as before and always, the greatest of these is love.

---

55. From Edgar's response in D. Bohm, S. Kelly, and E. Morin, "Order, Disor-der, and the Absolute: an Experiment in Dialogue," *World Futures* 46.4 (1996): 223–37.

References

Arctic News. Accessed August 7, 2015. http://arctic-news.blogspot. com/

Armitage, D. "What's the Big Idea? Intellectual History and the Longue Durée." *History of European Ideas* 38.4 (2012): 493–507. Accessed May 2, 2020. http://dx.doi.org/10.1080/01916599.2012 .714635.

Assman, J. "Cultural Memory and the Myth of the Axial Age." In Bellah and Joas, *The Axial Age and its Consequences*, 366–408.

Aurobindo. *Synthesis of Yoga.* Pondicherry: Sri Aurobindo Ashram Press, 1999.

Bache, C. *Dark Night, Early Dawn.* Albany: SUNY Press, 2000.

Baskin, K. and D.M. Bondarenko. *The Axial Ages of World History: Lessons for the 21st Century.* Litchfield Park: Emergent Publications, 2014.

Baumer, F. L. Van. *Main Currents Of Western Thought: Readings In Western Europe Intellectual History From The Middle Ages To The Present.* New Haven: Yale UP, 1978.

Bellah, R. *Religion in Human Evolution: From the Paleolithic to the Axial Age.* Cambridge, MA: Harvard UP, 2011.

Bellah, R. and H. Joas, editors. *The Axial Age and its Consequences.* Cambridge, MA: Harvard UP, 2012.

Bendell, J. "Deep Adaptation: A Map for Navigating Climate Tragedy." *Institute of Leadership and Sustainability.* July 27, 2018. Accessed May 3, 2020. https://www.lifeworth.com/deepadaptation.pdf.

———. "Hope and Vision in the Face of Collapse – The 4th R of Deep Adaptation." January 9, 2019. Accessed May 3, 2020. https://jembendell.com/2019/01/09/hope-and-vision-in-the-face-of-collapse-the-4th-r-of-deep-adaptation/.

Berry, T. *The Sacred Universe: Earth, Spirituality, and Religion in the Twenty-First Century.* New York: Columbia UP, 2009.

Berthrong, J.H. "Neo-Confucian Philosophy." *Internet Encyclopedia of Philosophy.* Accessed September 6, 2015. http://www.iep.utm. edu/neo-conf/#SH5a.

Bezold, C. "Jim Dator's Alternative Futures and the Path to IAF's Aspirational Futures."*Journal of Futures Studies* 14.2 (2009): 123–34.

Blake, W. *The Letters of William Blake with Related Documents.* 3rd ed. Ed. Geoffrey Keynes, Kt. Oxford.: Clarendon Press, 1980.

Blue Cross Blue Shield. "Major Depression: The Impact on Overall Health." May 10, 2018. Accessed May 3, 2020. https://www.

bcbs.com/sites/default/files/file-attachments/health-of-america-report/
HoA_Major_Depression_Report.pdf.

Boethius. *The Consolation of Philosophy*. Translated by W.V. Cooper.
Grand Rapids: J. M. Dent, 1902.

Bohm, D., S. Kelly, and E. Morin. "Order, Disorder, and the Absolute:
an Experiment in Dialogue." *World Futures* 46.4 (1996): 223–37.

Brons, L. "Fictionalism—or: Vaihinger, Scheffler, and Kübler-Ross at
the End of the World." *F=ma*. October 22, 2018. Accessed May 3,
2020. http://www.lajosbrons.net/blog/fictionalism-about-the-fu-
ture/.

Brown, S. "50 years after Theology of Hope, Jürgen Moltmann's vision
continues to inspire," in *World Council of Churches*, 03 February
2016. Accessed October 21, 2020 https://www.oikoumene.org/
news/50-years-after-theology-of-hope-jurgen-moltmanns-vision-
continues-to-inspire#_ftn2

Buffybison. "Can We Heal this Planet/Stop Climate Change with Law
of Attraction?" Reddit. June 12, 2019. Accessed May 3, 2020.
https://www.reddit.com/r/lawofattraction/comments/bzaejf/can_we_
heal_this_planetstop_climate_change_with/.

Casanova, J. "Religion, the Axial Age, and Secular Modernity in Bellah's Theory of Religious Evolution." In Bellah and Joas, *The Axial Age and its Consequences*, 191–221.

Ceballos, G., P. Ehrlich, et al. "Accelerated Modern Human–induced
Species Losses: Entering the Sixth Mass Extinction." *Sciences Advances* 1.5 (June 5, 2015).

Chaisson, E. "Big History's Risk and Challenge," *Expositions* 8.1
(2014): 85–95. Accessed June 24, 2015. https://www.cfa.harvard.
edu/~ejchaisson/reprints/Expositions_BH.pdf.

Christian, D. *Maps of Time: An Introduction to Big History*. Berkeley:
University of California Press, 2004.

Clarke, B. "Autopoiesis and the Planet." In *Impasses of the Post-Global: Theory in the Era of Climate Change*, Vol. 2, edited by Henry
Sussman, 58–75. Ann Arbor: University of Michigan, 2012.

Cooper, J.W. *Panentheism: The Other God of the Philosophers: From
Plato to the Present*. Grand Rapids: Baker Academic, 2006.

Cousins, E. *Christ of the 21st Century*. Rockport: Element Books, 1992.

Cragwall, R. "All Beliefs Are Self Imposed—Even Climate Change."
The Law of the Promised. June 9, 2017. Accessed May 3, 2020.
https://thelawthepromisecom.wordpress.com/2017/06/09/all-beliefs-
are-self-imposed-even-climate-change/

Crist, E. and H.B. Rinker. *Gaia in Turmoil: Climate Change, Biodepletion, and Earth Ethics in an Age of Crisis*. Cambridge, MA: MIT
Press, 2010.

Cusa, N. *Nicholas of Cusa: Selected Spiritual Writings*, Trans. H. Lawrence Bond. New York: Paulist Press, 1997.

Damasio, A. *The Feeling of What Happens: Body and Emotion in the Making of Consciousness*. Boston: Mariner Books, 2000.

Dante. *The Divine Comedy, Revised Edition*, Trans. James Finn Cotter. Forum Italicum, 2000.

———. Mandelbaum translation: https://digitaldante.columbia.edu/dante/divine-comedy/inferno/inferno-3/

Dogen. *Moon In a Dewdrop: Writings of Zen Master Dogen*. New York: North Point Press, 1995.

Donald, M. "An Evolutionary Approach to Culture: Implications for the Study of the Axial Age." In Bellah and Joas, *The Axial Age and its Consequences*, 47–76.

Ducharme, J. "US Suicide Rates Are the Highest They've Been Since World War II." TIME. June 20, 2019. Accessed May 3, 2020. https://time.com/5609124/us-suicide-rate-increase/

Ehrenreich, B. "There's Only One Antidote for Climate Despair—Climate Revolt." *The Nation*. September 9, 2019. Accessed May 3, 2020. https://www.thenation.com/article/extinction-rebellion/

Elliot, L. and E. Pilkington. "New Oxfam Report Says Half of Global Wealth Held by the 1%." *The Guardian*. January 19, 2015. Accessed August 2, 2015. http://www.theguardian.com/business/2015/jan/19/global-wealth-oxfam-inequality-davos-economic-summit-switzerland

Ellul, J. *The Technological Society*. New York: Vintage Books, 1954.

Esbjörn-Hargens, S. and M. Zimmerman. *Integral Ecology: Uniting Multiple Perspectives on the Natural World*. Boston and London: Integral Books, 2009.

Fox, M. "Major Depression on the Rise Among Everyone, New Data Shows." NBC News. May 10, 2018. Accessed May 3, 2020. https://www.nbcnews.com/health/health-news/major-depression-rise-among-everyone-new-data-shows-n873146

Gebser, J. *The Ever-present Origin*. Translated by N. Barstad. Athens: Ohio UP, 1986.

Global Footprint Network. Accessed April 25, 2020. http://www.footprintnetwork.org/en/index.php/GFN/page/world_footprint/

Graeber, D. "Savage Capitalism is Back—and It will not Tame Itself." The Guardian. May 30, 2014. Accessed September 21, 2015. https://www.theguardian.com/commentisfree/2014/may/30/savage-capitalism-back-radical-challenge

Grim, J. and M.E. Tucker. *Ecology and Religion*. Washington, DC: Island Press, 2014.

Grof, S. *Beyond the Brain: Birth, Death and Transcendence in Psycho-*

therapy. Albany: SUNY Press, 1985.

———. *The Adventure of Self-Discovery: Dimensions of Consciousness and New Perspectives in Psychotherapy and Inner Exploration.* Albany: SUNY Press, 1988.

———. "Modern Consciousness Research and Human Survival." In *Human Survival and Consciousness Evolution,* edited by S. Grof with M.L. Valier, 57–79. Albany: SUNY Press, 1988.

———. *The Way of the Psychonaut: Encyclopedia for Inner Journeys.* Two Volumes. Multidisciplinary Association for Psychedelic Studies, 2020.

Hamilton, C. *Defiant Earth: The Fate of Humans in the Anthropocene.* Cambridge: Polity, 2017.

Harding, S. "Earth System Science and Gaian Science." Earth System Science. Proceedings of the International School on Earth and Planetary Sciences. Siena: University of Siena, 2001. Schumacher College. Accessed May 2, 2020. https://www.schumachercollege.org.uk/learning-resources/earth-system-science-and-gaian-science

Havel, V. *Disturbing the Peace: A Conversation with Karel Huizdala.* New York: Vintage Books, 1991.

Hawken, P. *Blessed Unrest: How the Largest Social Movement in History Is Restoring Grace, Justice, and Beauty to the World.* New York: Penguin Books, 2008.

Hegel, G.W.F. *The Phenomenology of Spirit.* Oxford UP, 1981.

———. *Preface and Introduction to the Phenomenology of Mind,* Edited, with an introduction, by Lawrence S. Stepelevich. New York: Macmillan/Library of Liberal Arts, 1990.

Hillman, J. "Anima mundi: The return of the soul to the world." *Spring* (1982): 71–93.

Hine, D. "After We Stop Pretending." The Dark Mountain Project. April 22, 2019. Accessed May 3, 2020. https://dark-mountain.net/after-we-stop-pretending/

Holton, G.J. *Thematic Origins of Scientific Thought: Kepler to Einstein.* Cambridge: Harvard UP, 1998.

Ingham, J. "Bolivia's Offerings to Mother Earth." BBC News. October 28, 2007. Accessed May 3, 2020. http://news.bbc.co.uk/2/hi/programmes/from_our_own_correspondent/7062647.stm

Ingram, C. "Facing Extinction." March 2020. Accessed May 3, 2020. http://www.catherineingram.com/facingextinction/

James, W. "On Some Hegelisms." In *William James: Writings 1878–1899,* edited by G.E. Meyers. New York: Library of America, 1992.

———. *The Varieties of Religious Experience.* New York: Penguin Books, 1982.

Jaspers, K. *The Origin and Goal of History.* New Haven: Yale UP, 1968.

Johnson, J. *Seeing Through the World: Jean Gebser and Integral Consciousness.* Seattle: Revelore Press, 2019.

Jung, C.G. *Psychological Types (The Collected Works of C.G. Jung Vol. 6).* Princeton UP, 1976.

———. *Aion: Researches into the Phenomenology of the Self (The Collected Works of C.G. Jung Vol. 9 Part 2).* Princeton UP, 1979.

———. and W.E. Pauli. *The Interpretation of Nature and the Psyche.* New York: Ishi Press, 2012.

Keller, C. *From a Broken Web: Separation, Sexism, and Self.* Boston: Beacon Press, 1988.

Kelly, S. *Coming Home: The Birth and Transformation of the Planetary Era.* Great Barrington: Lindisfarne Books, 2010.

———. "Evolutionary Panentheism for the Planetary Era: A Gallery of Images." Seven Pillars House of Wisdom. November 10, 2009. Accessed May 3, 2020. http://www.sevenpillarshouse.org/article/evolutionary_panentheism_for_the_planetary_era/

———. "Five Principles of Integral Ecology." In Mickey, Kelly, and Robbert, *The Variety of Integral Ecologies,* 189–227.

———. *Individuation and the Absolute: Hegel, Jung, and the Path Toward Wholeness.* New York: Paulist Press, 1993.

———. "Integral Ecology and Edgar Morin's Paradigm of Complexity." In Mickey, Kelly, and Robbert, *The Variety of Integral Ecologies,* 81–101.

———. "Integral Time and the Varieties of Post-Mortem Survival." *Integral Review* 4.1 (2008): 5–30. Accessed May 3, 2020. http://integral-review.org/integral-time-and-the-varieties-of-post-mortem-survival/

Kelly, S. and J. Macy. "The Great Turning: Reconnecting Through Collapse." In *Deep Adaptation: Pathways through Climate Chaos,* edited by J. Bendell and R. Read. Forthcoming.

Klein, N. *This Changes Everything: Capitalism vs. the Climate.* New York: Simon & Schuster, 2014.

Korten, D. *The Great Turning: From Empire to Earth Community.* Bloomfield: Kumarian Press, 2006.

Latour, B. *Facing Gaia: Eight Lectures on the New Climate Regime.* Cambridge: Polity Press, 2017.

Lent, J. "Our Actions Create the Future: A Response to Jem Bendell." Patterns of Meaning. April 11, 2019. Accessed May 3, 2020. https://patternsofmeaning.com/2019/04/11/our-actions-create-the-future-a-response-to-jem-bendell/

Lovelock, J. *Gaia: A New Look at Life on Earth.* Oxford: Oxford UP, 2016.

Macy, J. *World as Lover, World as Self: Courage for Global Justice and Ecological Renewal*. Berkeley: Parallax Press, 2007.

Macy, J. and C. Johnstone. *Active Hope: How to Face the Mess We're in without Going Crazy*. New World Library, 2012.

Marvel, K. "We Need Courage, Not Hope, To Face Climate Change." *On Being*. March 1, 2018. Accessed May 3, 2020. https://onbeing. org/blog/kate-marvel-we-need-courage-not-hope-to-face-climate-change/

McDermott, R. *The Essential Aurobindo: Writings of Sri Aurobindo*. Lindisfarne Books, 2001.

Merchant, C. *The Death of Nature: Women, Ecology and the Scientific Revolution*. San Francisco: HarperOne, 1990.

Mickey, S., S. Kelly, and A. Robbert, editors. *The Variety of Integral Ecologies: Nature, Culture, and Knowledge in the Planetary Era*. Albany: SUNY Press, 2017.

Mooney, C. "Scientists Confirm that the Arctic Could Become a Major New Source of Carbon Emissions." *The Washington Post*. April 8, 2015.

Morin, E. *La Méthode 1: La Nature de la Nature*. Paris: Éditions du Seuil, 1977.

——. *La Méthode 2: La Vie de la Vie*. Paris: Éditions du Seuil, 1980.

——. *La Méthode 3: La Connaissance de la Connaissance*. Paris: Éditions du Seuil, 1986.

——. *La Méthode 5: L'Identité Humaine*. Paris: Éditions du Seuil, 2001.

——. *La Méthode 6: Éthique*. Paris: Éditions du Seuil, 2004.

——. "RE: From Prefix to Paradigm." *World Futures* 61.4 (2005): 254–67.

Morin, E. with B. Kerne. *Homeland Earth: A Manifesto for the New Millennium*. New York: Hampton Press, 1999.

——. *On Complexity*. New York: Hampton Press, 2008.

Morton, T. *The Ecological Thought*. Cambridge, MA: Harvard UP, 2010.

Mutasa, C. "Global Apartheid." Global Policy Forum. September 9, 2004. Accessed August 4, 2015. https://www.globalpolicy.org/ component/content/article/210/44769.html

Nietzsche, F. *The Will to Power*. Trans. W. Kaufmann and R. J. Hollingdale. New York: Random House, 1967.

Olivetti, K. "Dimensions of the Psyche: A Conversation with Stanislav Grof, M.D., and Richard Tarnas, Ph.D." *The Jung Journal: Culture and Psyche* 9.4 (2015): 98–124.

Owens, L. *Jung in Love: The* Mysterium *in* Liber Novus. Los Angeles: Gnosis Archive Books, 2015.

Panikkar, R. *The Rhythm of Being: The Unbroken Trinity*. The Gifford Lectures. Maryknoll: Orbis Books, 2013.

———. *The Vedic Experience*. London: Darton, Longman & Todd, 1979.

Pessoa, L. "Cognition and Emotion." Scholarpedia. Accessed May 2, 2020. doi:10.4249/scholarpedia.4567

Pimm, S. L., C. N. Jenkins, et al. "The Biodiversity of Species and Their Rates of Extinction, Distribution, and Protection." *Science* 344.6187 (May 30, 2014).

Pogge, T. and K. Bhatt. "Thomas Pogge on the Past, Present and Future of Global Poverty." *Truthout*. May 29, 2011. Accessed August 2, 2015. http://www.truth-out.org/news/item/792:thomas-pogge-on-the-past-present-and-future-of-global-poverty

Richardson, J.H. "When the End of Human Civilization Is Your Day Job." Esquire. July 20, 2018. Accessed May 20, 2020. https://www.esquire.com/news-politics/a36228/ballad-of-the-sad-climatologists-0815/

Rifkin, J. *The Empathic Civilization: The Race to Global Consciousness in a World in Crisis*. New York: Tarcher/Penguin, 2009.

Rilke, R.M. "Buddha in Glory." In *Ahead of All Parting: The Selected Poetry and Prose of Rainer Maria Rilke*. Trans. Stephen Mitchell. New York: Modern Library, 1995.

Russell, P. "Blind Spot: The Unforeseen End of Accelerating Change." Accessed May 3, 2020. https://www.peterrussell.com/blindspot/blindspot.pdf

Sabetta, G. "Panikkar's Intercultural Challenge: Philosophical, Theological and Political Aspects." Accessed August 7, 2015. https://www.academia.edu/9828052/Panikkars_Intercultural_and_Inter-religious_Challenge

Schellnhuber, H.J. "Discourse: Earth System Analysis—The Scope of the Challenge." Accessed May 2, 2020. http://edoc.gfz-potsdam.de/pik/get/1224/0/15809de6c77a70f38cb34da38db533f6/1224.pdf

Schneider, S. et al. *Scientists Debate Gaia: The Next Century*. Cambridge, MA: MIT Press, 2008.

Segall, M. and R. Tarnas. "Disenchantment, Disenchantment, and Reenchantment." Accessed August 7, 2015. http://footnotes2plato.com/2014/01/06/disenchantment-misenchantment-and-re-enchantment-a-dialogue-with-richard-tarnas/

Sengupta, S. "Protesting Climate Change, Young People Take to Streets in a Global Strike." *New York Times*. September 20, 2019. Accessed May 3, 2020. https://www.nytimes.com/2019/09/20/climate/global-climate-strike.html

Servigne, P. and Stevens. *How Everything Can Collapse*. Cambridge: Polity Press, 2020.

Sheldrake, R. *The Presence of the Past: Morphic Resonance and the Habits of Nature*. New York: Times Books, 1988.

Spretnak, C. *States of Grace: The Recovery of Meaning in the Postmodern Age*. San Francisco: Harper San Francisco, 1993.

Stengers, I. "The Intrusion of Gaia." In *In Catastrophic Times: Resisting the Coming Barbarism*. Trans. Andrew Goffey. Open Humanities Press, 2015.

Stone, J. *Original Enlightenment and the Transformation of Medieval Japanese Buddhism*. Honolulu: University of Hawai'i Press, 1999.

Swimme, B. and M.E. Tucker. *Journey of the Universe*. New Haven: Yale UP, 2011.

Swimme, B. and T. Berry. *The Universe Story: From the Primordial Flaring Forth to the Ecozoic Era—A Celebration of the Unfolding of the Cosmos*. San Francisco: HarperCollins, 1992.

Táíwò, O. and Beba Cibralic. "The Case for Climate Reparations". *FP Insider Access*. October 10, 2020. Accessed October 17, 2020. https://foreignpolicy.com/2020/10/10/case-for-climate-reparations-crisis-migration-refugees-inequality/

Tarnas, R. "Is the Modern Psyche Undergoing a Rite of Passage?" Cosmos and Psyche, 2001. Accessed May 3, 2020. https://cosmosandpsyche.files.wordpress.com/2013/05/revision-rite-of-passage.pdf

———. *The Passion of the Western Mind: Understanding the Ideas That Have Shaped Our World View*. New York: Harmony Books, 1991.

Taylor, C. *Sources of the Self: The Making of the Modern Identity*. Cambridge, MA: Harvard UP, 1989/1996.

———. "What was the Axial Revolution?" In Bellah and Joas, *The Axial Age and its Consequences*, 30–46.

Thunberg, G. "'Our House is on Fire': Greta Thunberg, 16, Urges Leaders to Act on Climate." *The Guardian*. January 25, 2019. Accessed May 3, 2020. https://www.theguardian.com/environment/2019/jan/25/our-house-is-on-fire-greta-thunberg16-urges-leaders-to-act-on-climate

Voegelin, E. *The Ecumenic Age*. Columbia: University of Missouri Press, 1974.

Voros, J. "Profiling 'Threshold 9': Using Big History as a Framework for Thinking about the Contours of the Coming Global Future." In *Evolution: Development within Big History, Evolutionary and World-system Paradigms*, edited by L.E. Grinin and A.V. Korotayev, 119–42. Volgograd, Russia: Uchitel, 2013.

Wallace-Wells, D. *The Uninhabitable Earth: Life After Warming*. New York: Tim Duggan Books, 2019.

Watts, J. "We Have 12 years to Limit Climate Change Catastrophe, Warns UN." *The Guardian.* October 8, 2018. Accessed May 3, 2020. https://www.theguardian.com/environment/2018/oct/08/global-warming-must-not-exceed-15c-warns-landmark-un-report

Whitehead, A.N. *Process and Reality.* New York: MacMillan, 1978.

Wilber, K. *A Brief History of Everything.* Boston: Shambhala,1996.

———. "The Developmental Spectrum and Psychopathology: Part I, Stages and Types of Pathology." *The Journal of Transpersonal Psychology* 16.1 (1984): 75–118.

———. "The Developmental Spectrum and Psychopathology: Part II, Treatment Modalities." *The Journal of Transpersonal Psychology* 16.1 (1984): 137–66.

———. *The Eye of Spirit: An Integral Vision for a World Gone Slightly Mad.* In *The Collected Works of Ken Wilber.* Volume Seven. Boston: Shambhala, 2000.

———. *Integral Psychology: Consciousness, Spirit, Psychology, Therapy.* Boston: Shambhala 2000.

———. *Integral Spirituality: A Startling New Role for Religion in the Modern and Postmodern World.* Boston and London: Integral Books, 2007.

———. *Sex, Ecology, Spirituality.* In *The Collected Works of Ken Wilber.* Volume Six. Boston: Shambhala, 2000.

———. *Up from Eden: A Transpersonal View of Human Evolution.* In *The Collected Works of Ken Wilber.* Volume Two. Boston: Shambhala, 1999.

Woodbury, Z. "Planetary Hospice: Rebirthing Planet Earth." Accessed May 3, 2020. https://guymcpherson.com/wp-content/uploads/2014/03/Planetary-Hospice.pdf

Yardley J. and L. Goodstein. "Pope Francis, in Sweeping Encyclical, Calls for Swift Action on Climate Change." *New York Times.* June 18, 2015. Accessed June 24, 2015. https://www.nytimes.com/2015/06/19/world/europe/pope-francis-in-sweeping-encyclical-calls-for-swift-action-on-climate-change.html

Index

215

About the Author

SEAN KELLY is professor of Philosophy, Cosmology, and Consciousness at the California Institute of Integral Studies (CIIS). He is the author of *Coming Home: The Birth and Transformation of the Planetary Era*, co-editor of *The Variety of Integral Ecologies: Nature, Culture, and Knowledge in the Planetary Era*, and co-translator of Edgar Morin's *Homeland Earth: A Manifesto for the New Millennium*. Along with his academic work, Sean teaches t'ai chi and is a facilitator of the group process Work that Reconnects developed by Joanna Macy.